A School Administrator's Guide to Early Childhood Programs

A School Administrator's Guide to Early Childhood Programs

Second Edition

Lawrence J. Schweinhart

High/Scope® Educational Research Foundation

With a Foreword by
Paul D. Houston
Executive Director
American Association of School Administrators

Ypsilanti, Michigan

Published by
HIGH/SCOPE® PRESS
A division of the High/Scope Educational Research Foundation
600 North River Street
Ypsilanti, Michigan 48198-2898
PHONE (734) 485-2000, FAX (734) 485-0704
Web site: *www.highscope.org,* E-Mail: *press@highscope.org*

Editor: Linda Koopmann
Cover design, text design: Judy Seling of Seling Design

Library of Congress Cataloging-in-Publication Data

Schweinhart, L. J. (Lawrence J.), 1947-
  A school administrator's guide to early childhood programs / Lawrence
J. Schweinhart.-- 2nd ed.
        p. cm.
Includes bibliographical references (p.   ).
  ISBN 1-57379-205-5 (Soft cover : alk. paper)
  1. Early childhood education--United States. 2. Education,
Preschool--United States. I. Title.
  LB1139.25.S394 2004
  372.21'0973--dc22
                                2003024708

The High/Scope Educational Research Foundation is an independent, nonprofit center for research, development, and training in education and human development, with primary emphasis on early childhood development programs. Founded in 1970, today it maintains a staff of 60 and an annual budget of $7 million from public and private sources.

Printed in the United States of America

10 9 8 7 6 5 4 3 2 1

CONTENTS

LIST OF TABLES AND FIGURES

TABLES

FIGURES

FOREWORD

Paul D. Houston
Executive Director
American Association of School Administrators

It has been said that it's not where you start but where you finish that counts. But sadly, where and how children start often determines where and how they finish. For this reason, a good start is so important to children—particularly those children who need every advantage to overcome difficult early years.

Early childhood programs may be new to public schools, but they meet a long-unfilled need in public education. The organization of schools into grades many years ago had the effect of making several profound, enduring statements about schooling. One was that students would be grouped by year of birth, with those born in a 12-month time span grouped together. The second profound statement concerned the beginning of schooling—that the first grade of schooling would be designated specifically for 6-year-olds. These decisions have done more to shape the institution of schooling than most if not all the ideas of leading educational thinkers over the nation's history.

The reason for setting age 6 as the time for the first grade was presumably the emergent abilities of 6-year-olds to focus on and master the symbol-processing skills of reading, writing, and arithmetic that are basic to further education in ideas.

Thus, when Froebel invented the kindergarten in the mid-1800s, this educational innovation focused on 3- to 5-year-olds in Germany, then 5-year-olds alone in the one-year-at-a-time educational culture of the United States. Kindergarten became the year of the "children's garden" that preceded the well-established first grade of schooling. Even the name "garden" signaled the shift from the sensory richness of plants and greenery to the abstractions of schooling. A century and a half later, kindergarten at age 5 has become universally established throughout the U.S., practically as well established as grades 1 through 12.

In the early 1960s, a couple of new ideas about early childhood education emerged—the idea that education began even earlier than kindergarten and the idea that early childhood education could make important contributions to improving the lives of young children living in poverty. David Weikart in Michigan, Susan Gray in Tennessee, and Marty Deutsch in New York began demonstration programs for 3- and 4-year-olds and set up scientific designs to examine their effects. Then came the national Head Start program in the mid-1960s. Two decades later, the states followed suit, so that today almost all states invest in preschool or Head Start programs.

Because Head Start was part of the Office of Economic Opportunity as well as the civil rights movement in general, it did not simply become part of the nation's public schools (although it sometimes did); by and large Head Start became part of community action agencies, the fleet ships of President Johnson's War on Poverty. Community action agencies were institutions founded almost in opposition to public schools that had been insensitive to some people's civil rights. When President Jimmy Carter thought to move Head Start into the new U.S. Department of Education, the resistance inherent in the rival incipient institution of community action agencies prevailed, and Head Start remained outside of the Department of Education.

Now President George W. Bush seeks to remake Head Start by focusing its attention on literacy and mathematics outcomes and by regularly assessing children. At the same time he seeks to make Head Start programs more fully part of America's public schools by shifting from direct federal funding to state-mediated funding with federal guidelines rather than regulations. Thus, Head Start programs would join their sister state preschool programs that are mostly based in public schools. However the current Head Start re-authorization turns out, the movement of preschool programs into the nation's public schools is definite and probably irreversible. After all, public schools are by far America's dominant institution for the education of young people, with the modest exceptions of private schools and Head Start. The question is not whether Head Start will merge into the public schools, but how and at what rate.

Nonetheless, Head Start and child care programs have developed an institutional history mostly outside the public schools. This historical legacy is broadly identified with the National Association for the Education of Young Children and its unusually successful espousal of "developmentally appropriate practice."

It would be one thing if the child development approach interfered with children's optimal development into good students and good citizens. But the program and research of the High/Scope Educational Research Foundation and others shows that far from interfering with optimal development, the child development approach in fact can contribute to children's development in strikingly positive ways. Indeed, in the High/Scope longitudinal studies, a good preschool program in which 3- and 4-year-old children are active participants in their own education propels them on their way to becoming more successful and responsible, not only in their early childhood years but throughout their lives.

As school administrators and teachers seek to assist parents in the rearing of their young children, our challenge is to give children the kinds of programs they deserve—programs that enable children to become active participants in their own education for the first time in their young lives: programs with teachers well-versed in child development and well-trained in valid models of early childhood education who know what they need to do; programs that maintain generous staff-child ratios so staff can give young children the attention they need; and programs that treat parents as genuine and full partners in their young children's education, through regular home visits and regular gatherings focused on their joint challenge.

The secret to powerful education at any level is that it becomes meaningful and engaging to the learner. One of the great strengths of early childhood education is that it, above all other levels in the educational process, has best modeled this ideal. In our rush for accountability and excellence in academics, we cannot afford to forget that personal accountability and individual excellence are the goals of any great education.

That is the vision of early childhood programs advanced by this volume, and it is the vision of early childhood programs that makes them worth doing. To do any less would shortchange our young children—our nation's most promising and most vulnerable resource. To do anything less would ensure that where our children finish is not their most promising destination.

PREFACE

If you are an elementary school principal or some other type of school administrator, this guide presents the information you need to develop and maintain good early childhood education programs for three- to five-year-olds in your school. In addition, it presents the educational principles that are relevant not only to early childhood programs but also to the elementary grades. It will help you to

- Recognize good early childhood education

- Explain the rationale for early education to parents and others

- Provide appropriate administrative support and evaluation for early childhood programs

- Integrate new ideas about early childhood education into your existing views of education

In this guide, three key questions are considered:

1. What constitutes a good early childhood program? A good early childhood program should employ an educational model based on principles of child development, one that recognizes young children's intellectual, social, and physical needs and encourages children to initiate their own learning activities within a supportive environment. It requires an enthusiastic and knowledgeable administrator together with a teaching staff well trained in early childhood development and participating in ongoing inservice training. Each class should have a teacher, an aide, and an enrollment limit of 16–20; and teaching staffs need time set aside for planning and evaluation. Parents should be active partners in the education process, and the noneducational needs of the child and family, such as child care, health, and nutrition, should be considered.

2. What is your role? As an elementary school principal or other administrator, you should understand the goals of your educational model and help your teaching staff accomplish these goals and explain them to parents. Provide your teachers and aides with a systematic program of inservice training focused on child development principles and follow up to see that they apply these principles in the classroom. Make sure that evaluations of programs and teaching staff are consistent with the goals of your educational model.

3. What are the critical choices? Every administrator who is attempting to implement a good early childhood classroom, as well as an effective overall school program, grapples with some very important issues. What about postponing kindergarten entry for less-mature children? What about teacher-directed instruction in the basic skills? What about teaching reading to preschoolers? What about standardized achievement tests? What about the dangers of labeling young children by placing them in early childhood special education programs? This guide is designed to help you sort through these and related issues. It is written from a child development perspective, but considers other ideas about early childhood education as well.

I have tried to anticipate the most pressing questions and concerns of elementary school principals and other school administrators about early childhood programs. If you have questions about early childhood programs that are not addressed in this booklet, first visit the High/Scope Web site at *www.highscope.org.* If after reviewing the material presented there you still have questions, please e-mail me at *lschweinhart@ highscope.org,* or write to me at the High/Scope Educational Research Foundation, 600 North River Street, Ypsilanti, MI 48198.

The first edition of this booklet, published in 1988, resulted from a collaboration between the High/Scope Educational Research Foundation and the National Association of Elementary School Principals—in particular, Samuel Sava, the organization's former executive director; Edna May Merson, president from 1986 to 1987; and the other members of its Early Childhood Advisory Panel: Robert Anastasi, Neil Chance, Carolyn Cummings, Greer Gladstone, Edward Keller, Helen Martin, Neil Shipman, and Romaine Thomas. This edition continues to profit from their wisdom.

Fifteen years have passed since this booklet was first published. It is gratifying that some readers have found it useful enough to warrant a revision. Revising it has been an interesting study of stability and change in America's thinking about early childhood education over that period of time. The basic structure of the booklet has remained the same—the rationale for good early childhood education, the definition of good early childhood education, and the way early childhood education fits into schools. But new studies have been conducted, including some we have conducted, and the case for early childhood programs and their quality is stronger than ever. We have refined our thinking about children's active learning, concerned that some have taken it to mean more activity than learning, so in this edition we refer to children's *planning of learning activities,* to emphasize their purposefulness. We have replaced the section on various other educational approaches with a chapter on the school readiness movement. This movement is clearly the most important set of ideas affecting early childhood programs and their relationship with the schools today.

A most striking part of the revision process has been the emergence of the World Wide Web as a research tool. When I wrote this book 15 years ago, the Web was virtually nonexistent for general research purposes. Now, it has become indispensable; references to Web addresses pepper the list of references and resource organizations in this second edition. It seems likely that even this high level of access to materials through the Web is transitional. Indeed, I expect in my lifetime to see the Web become the nearly exclusive tool for research into the ideas and findings of others.

In similar fashion, early childhood education has become more and more a part of the mainstream. In 2002, Head Start served 905,235 children, twice as many as in 1988, with funding of $6.3 billion—3.8 times as much as in 1988 even after inflation (Head Start Bureau, 2002). In 2000, 43 states funded prekindergarten programs that served about 725,000 children, spending $2.1 billion, three times as much as in 1992 (Cauthen, Knitzer, & Ripple, 2000; Schulman, Blank, & Ewen, 1999). Some states are now funding programs open to all 4-year-olds without qualification. Throughout this expansion, the principal challenge is the same—to maintain the high quality and broad child development focus of all early childhood programs. If this booklet contributes in some small way to meeting these goals, its purpose has been achieved.

Lawrence J. Schweinhart
March, 2004

A School Administrator's Guide to Early Childhood Programs

1

⌒

The Rationale for Good Early Childhood Education

Today, numerous carefully designed experimental research studies point out the great potential of high-quality early childhood education, especially for children at risk of school failure. In this chapter, we present these research results in straightforward, nontechnical language, so that you can present them to parents, teachers, and others.

What Good Early Childhood Programs Can Accomplish

In one of our experimental studies of the effects of early childhood education, the High/Scope Perry Preschool study (Schweinhart, Barnes, & Weikart, 1993), we randomly assigned children at risk of school failure either to a preschool program group that attended the High/Scope Perry Preschool Program or to a no-program group that attended no preschool program; the two groups were almost exactly alike in background characteristics. In assessing effects of the preschool program, we considered subsequent differences favoring the program group to be *program benefits* and would have considered differences favoring the no-program group to be *program costs*. In fact, from the time study participants were 4 years old up to the time they were 27 years old, we consistently found program *benefits,* not costs; we are now analyzing data collected from participants at age 40 to discover if program benefits extend even further into adult life.

The study so far has revealed very interesting results. The program not only provided an immediate benefit to parents in the form of supplemental child care but also produced short-term benefits that included improvements in children's intellectual and social skills at elementary-school entry *and* long-term social benefits that included reduced risks of educational disability, school drop-out, crime, unemployment, and dependence on welfare assistance. These long-term social benefits resulted in less need for various costly public services, a significant long-term financial benefit for taxpayers. (Appendix A contains more information on this cost-benefit analysis and other findings of the High/Scope Perry Preschool study.)

As might be expected, ours are not the only studies reaching these conclusions. Many other studies have verified the short-term effects of good early childhood development programs, and a few others besides ours have looked for and found long-term effects. In addition to ours, the long-term studies we consider here are the Abecedarian Project study in North Carolina; the Chicago Child-arent Centers study in Illinois; the Early Training study in Murfreesboro, Tennessee; a Head Start study in Rome, Georgia; and three independently conducted studies in New York State—the Harlem study, the Mother-Child Home study, and the New York Prekindergarten study. As shown in Table 1, these studies have discovered short-term, mid-term, and long-term effects of good early childhood programs for poor children. The evidence indicates that such programs

- **Do** help improve children's intellectual and social performance as they begin school. These short-term effects have been found in many studies of Head Start and other programs (McKey et al., 1985; McKey, 2003).

- **Probably** help children achieve greater school success. Seven studies found the mid-term effect of fewer poor children being placed in special education programs and having to repeat grade levels (Lazar, Darlington, Murray, Royce, & Snipper, 1982).

- **Can,** over the long-term, help young people achieve greater socioeconomic success and social responsibility, and in doing so, provide taxpayers with a handsome return on their investment (Campbell, Pungello, Miller-Johnson, Burchinal, & Ramey, 2001; Reynolds, Temple, Robertson, & Mann, 2001; Schweinhart et al., 1993).

Table 1
Significant Effects of Good Preschool Programs for Poor Children

Finding Study	Program Group	No-Program Group
IQ at elementary school entry		
Abecedarian	101	91
Early Training	96	86
Harlem	96	91
High/Scope Perry	94	83
Special education placements		
Abecedarian	25%	48%
Chicago Child-Parent Centers	14%	25%
Early Training	3%	29%
High/Scope Perry (mentally impaired only)	15%	34%
Mother-Child Home	14%	39%
New York Prekindergarten	2%	5%
Rome Head Start	11%	25%
Retentions in grade		
Abecedarian	31%	55%
Chicago Child-Parent Centers	23%	38%
Harlem	24%	45%
New York Prekindergarten	16%	21%
Reading achievement as teenager		
Abecedarian (age 15, standard scores)	94	89
High/Scope Perry (age 14, percentiles)	15th	9th
High/Scope Perry (age 19, average or better)	61%	38%
Math achievement as teenager		
Abecedarian (age 15, standard scores)	94	87
High/Scope Perry (age 14, percentiles)	13th	8th
High school graduates		
Abecedarian	67%	51%
Abecedarian: Ever enrolled in 4-year college	36%	13%
Chicago Child-Parent Centers	50%	39%
Early Training	70%	57%
High/Scope Perry	71%	54%
Rome Head Start	50%	33%
Arrests		
Chicago Child-Parent Centers (mean by 18)	0.5	0.8
High/Scope Perry (mean by 27)	2.3	4.6
Economic Return per Investment Dollar		
Carolina Abecedarian	$3.66	–
Chicago Child Parent Centers	$7.10	–
High/Scope Perry	$7.16	–

NOTE. Adapted from L. J. Schweinhart, H. V. Barnes, & D. P. Weikart, *Significant Benefits: The High/Scope Perry Preschool Study Through Age 27*, Monographs of the High/Scope Educational Research Foundation, 10 (Ypsilanti, MI: High/Scope Press, 1993), p. 14 and references cited therein. Each finding presented is statistically significant with a probability of less than .05 (1 out of 20) of occurring by chance.

The Head Start Family and Child Experiences Survey (FACES; McKey, 2003) is an ongoing look at Head Start children and families that examines some 6,000 children who entered the program in fall 1997 and fall 2000 (McKey, 2003). The study found that 27% of Head Start teachers have bachelor's degrees (Zill & Resnick, 2002a); observers rated 20% of the programs as excellent and 52% of them as good (Zill & Resnick, 2002b). The study identified various gains of Head Start children during their year in the program—in vocabulary, letter recognition, and early skills in writing and mathematics (Zill & Resnick, 2002b). It found that on average children come into the program knowing 4 letters and leave knowing 9 letters (McKey, 2003). The study also found that programs that use the High/Scope educational model contribute significantly to children's letter and word recognition skills and social skills (Zill, Resnick, Kim, O'Donnell, Sorongon, McKey, et al., 2003). However,

Young children need developmentally appropriate programs where they can exercise their emerging social, physical, and intellectual skills.

in a comparison of children's standard scores on the Peabody Picture Vocabulary Test in the FACES study and their scores in the High/Scope Perry Preschool Study, children gained 4 points in their Head Start year while children in High/Scope Perry gained 8 points in their first year and a total of 14 points in two years. To put it simply, the study found that Head Start programs are achieving some success, but could be doing more to help children reach their potential. The National Head Start Impact Study now under way promises to provide solid evidence about outcomes through random assignment of children to a Head Start or no–Head Start group. Random assignment is the most powerful research design for drawing conclusions about program effects.

As you have probably noted by now, the findings we have been discussing occurred in studies of children who live in poverty and are at risk of school failure. There is less evidence of early childhood program effectiveness for children who are not poor or otherwise at risk of school failure. There is some evidence, however, that a preschool program effect found for poor children would also apply to middle-class children, but to a lesser extent. An evaluation of the Brookline Early Education Project (BEEP) in Massachusetts found that after a comprehensive five-year early childhood program, the school problems of participating middle-class children were reduced somewhat. This study of mostly middle-class children had a preschool program group and a comparison group that did not participate in a preschool program. At the end of grade two, inappropriate classroom learning behavior was shown by 14% of BEEP's preschool group compared to 28% of its no-preschool group. Reading difficulties were identified in 19% of the preschool group versus 32% of the no-preschool group (Pierson, Walker, & Tivnan, 1984).

Research reveals that long-term benefits result only from *high-quality* early childhood development programs—ones characterized by a child development educational model, trained teaching staff, administrative leadership and curriculum support, small classes with a teacher and a teaching assistant, and systematic efforts to involve parents as partners. Such programs may be expensive, but their high return on the initial investment makes them more economical than a program that costs less initially but provides little or no return on the investment. It is probable that poorly funded programs with untrained staff provide nothing more than the immediate benefit of supplemental child care for families.

WHY CHILD-INITIATED LEARNING ACTIVITY IS IMPORTANT IN EARLY CHILDHOOD PROGRAMS

Today, the **early childhood field** recognizes the value of child-initiat-ed, developmentally appropriate activities in helping young children achieve their full potential. The 100,000-member National Association for the Education of Young Children (1997) has issued and regularly revises a position statement on developmentally appropriate practices

in early childhood programs from birth through age eight. The following are some of the principles identified:

- Children are active learners, drawing on direct physical and
  social experience as well as culturally transmitted knowledge
  to construct their own understandings of the world around
  them. (p. 13)

- Play is an important vehicle for children's social, emotional,
  and cognitive development, as well as a reflection of their
  development. (p. 14)

The following are some of the guidelines for decisions about
developmentally appropriate practice:

- Teachers create an intellectually engaging, responsive environment to promote each child's learning and development.

- Teachers provide children with opportunities to make meaningful choices and time to explore through active involvement.
  (p. 18)

The position statement makes the point that early childhood
practice profits more from both/and thinking, which includes both
alternatives of an apparent choice of practices, than from either/or
thinking, which chooses one practice to the exclusion of another.
For example,

- Children construct their own understanding of concepts, **and**
  they benefit from instruction by more competent peers and
  adults. (p. 23)

- Children benefit from engaging in self-initiated, spontaneous
  play **and** from teacher-planned and teacher-structured activities, projects, and experiences.

Parents, too, value children's independence and initiation of
their own activity. Duane Alwin (1984) of the University of Michigan's Institute for Social Research cited surveys finding that parents
in the 1950s highly valued obedience and good manners in their
children, while the next generation of parents preferred their children
to be independent and self-reliant. His analysis attributed the shift to

various changes in society: increases in the labor force participation of mothers and in the numbers of single-parent families and highly educated parents; increases in technological complexity and urbanization; the decrease in family size; and the change in attitudes towards childrearing.

The National Research Council and Institute of Medicine (2000) report *From Neurons to Neighborhoods* notes that "Children are active participants in their own development" (p. 27) and identifies self-regulation of emotions, attention, and executive functioning as major challenges of early childhood. It concludes, "The elements of early intervention programs that enhance social and emotional development are just as important as the components that enhance linguistic and cognitive competence" (p. 11).

RESEARCH GIVES US SOME ANSWERS

Research supporting the importance of child-initiated learning activity in early childhood programs comes from High/Scope's long-term Preschool Curriculum Comparison study. This study has examined the effects on young people through age 15 of three well-implemented programs based on different models of preschool education—Direct Instruction, High/Scope, and a typical nursery school curriculum (Schweinhart & Weikart, 1997). The Direct Instruction program emphasized intense, scripted, teacher-directed lessons, while the High/Scope and nursery school programs both emphasized child-initiated learning activity. The High/Scope model was based in part on joint planning by teachers and children, while the nursery school curriculum was based entirely on teachers striving to respond to the child's needs and interests.

The mean IQ of the children in the three programs, regardless of the educational model used, rose a remarkable 27 points during the first year of the programs, from 78 to 105, and remained in the normal range thereafter, with an average IQ of 94 at age 10. We therefore concluded at that time that *well-implemented* preschool programs had a positive effect regardless of which educational model was used.

Then, in a later stage of this study, we were quite surprised to discover that by age 23 only 6% of the High/Scope and nursery school groups had needed treatment for emotional impairment or disturbance during their schooling, as compared to 47% of the Direct Instruction group. Forty-three percent of the High/Scope group and 44% of the nursery school group had ever performed volunteer work, as compared to 11% of the Direct Instruction group, and only 10% of the High/Scope group had ever been arrested for a felony, as compared to 39% of the Direct Instruction group. This pattern strongly suggests that the High/Scope and nursery school programs took advantage of the early childhood opportunity to contribute importantly to children's social development, while the Direct Instruction program, focused exclusively on academic subject matter, did not.

Other studies of preschool educational models considered a variety of other short-term and long-term outcomes besides juvenile delinquency (Miller & Bizzell, 1984; Karnes, Schwedel, & Williams, 1983). These studies have found that in the short run, Direct Instruction preschool programs can improve IQs even more than other programs can, but that this is not the case in the long run. Karnes et al. (1983, pp. 157–160) found that by the end of high school, their Direct Instruction group did relatively poorly on several measures of school success. For example, high school graduation was achieved by 70% of their nursery school group, but only by 48% of their Direct Instruction group. However, by the end of high school none of these group differences were big enough to be statistically significant. Marcon (2002) examined the effects of three preschool models on children's school success up to five years later. Three-fourths of the 183 children had family incomes of up to 185% of the federal poverty level, qualifying them for subsidized school lunches. Although fewer children in academically directed preschool classes were later retained in grade, by the end of their sixth year in school their grades were significantly lower than those of children who had attended preschool classes that featured child-initiated learning activities (grade point averages of 2.25 for academically directed vs. 2.56 for child-initiated, adjusted for family income).

These studies all support the conclusion that a program of only direct instruction in the preschool years can lead to large, short-term improvements in children's intellectual performance and elementary-school achievement. However, they also present evidence that a program of only direct instruction in the preschool years is not as effective as other preschool programs over the long term in preventing school failure, high school dropout, and delinquent behavior.

The explanation for these negative long-term findings may be that the early childhood years are a developmental stage during which certain experiences help children develop the dispositions and skills by which they later avoid problematic or antisocial behavior. The Direct Instruction preschool approach seems to have failed to take full advantage of the opportunities that were available to positively influence the development of young children's social problem-solving skills. After all, its stated objectives were *academic,* while the other models in the comparisons included *social* objectives, such as children learning to share, get along with one another, and engage in conversation with one another and with teachers. Kamii (1986), applying psychologist Jean Piaget's theory

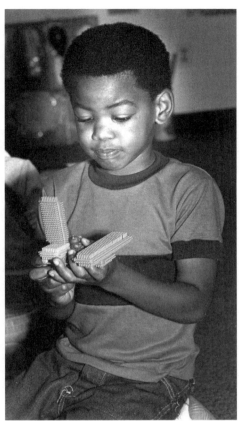

Programs providing children with opportunities to initiate their own learning activities have better long-term results than programs that rely mostly on teacher-directed activities.

of moral development to these findings, suggests that the Direct Instruction approach prevents children from developing autonomy, because the teacher is authoritarian and uses rewards and punishments, whereas the other two models encourage children's autonomy, because they allow teachers and children to discuss their points of view with one another.

FINDING THE BALANCE

In considering how to provide the best possible early childhood education experience for children, we must find the common ground between extremes. Young children will not just develop by themselves, as some would argue, but also should not be pushed to perform beyond their developing abilities, as others would have it. Young children are ready for appropriate educational experiences, but not for an exclusive diet of teacher-controlled lessons. We must consider both the child's emergent abilities and the child's interests in relation to proposed learning activities (Hunt, 1961).

One example of the current difficulty in grappling with this issue is the federal mandate to require children to develop specific literacy skills in Head Start. As a result of recent cries for educational reform in the public schools, students from Head Start through high school are being expected to demonstrate higher standards of academic performance. Many states and school districts have identified various academic skills that students are to master at each grade level. Establishing expectations for four-year-olds is not inappropriate in itself, but these expectations must take into account the nature of young children's thinking (Egertson, 1987). Young children's emerging abilities are best nurtured in programs that allow them to explore their environment freely under the purposeful guidance of teachers who have a good knowledge of early childhood development. With this basic principle in mind, let's consider what we know about high-quality early childhood education.

2

Good Early Childhood Education— The Hallmarks of Quality

People who are new to early childhood care and education often assume that its purpose is only to teach young children letters and numbers—the ABC's of our culture. While it is useful for young children to learn these symbols, they are only part of what young children should be learning to become good readers and mathematicians in their elementary school years. *Young children should be learning directly through their senses and through physical activities.* Furthermore, since an early childhood program is usually the child's first opportunity to learn from adults outside the family and within groups of children of similar age, it should enable the child to develop a positive attitude towards such learning. In this chapter, we explain how to operate a program of high quality that enables young children to learn as they learn best and to develop a sense of ownership of the learning process.

As an administrator of an early childhood program, you should know the answers to two important questions: What are the crucial differences between high-quality and low-quality early childhood programs? What are the critical components of high-quality early childhood programs?

We can look to experimental research on early childhood programs to help answer these questions, but such research does not answer them fully. As explained in Chapter I, most of this research compares children who attended a program and children who did not. Research of this design can tell us how successful programs are, but cannot pinpoint exactly which program elements are responsible for this success. We have considered program quality in light of findings from

several of these experimental studies—High/Scope's Preschool Curriculum Comparison study, one by Karnes, and one by Miller—that
have analyzed the effectiveness of various educational models. We
have also examined the findings of the growing tradition of child care
research (Ceglowski & Bacigalupa, 2002; Phillips, 1987). In the final
analysis, however, we have relied not only on these and other scientific studies to define high-quality programs but also on the varied program experiences that the early childhood community has accumulat-
ed over the years (Epstein et al., 1985). Our definition, presented in
Table 2, agrees with the accreditation criteria of the National Association for the Education of Young Children (1998).

It is important to note that a good early childhood program can
take place in any setting that has adequate financial and physical resources and an adequate number of qualified staff—in a private nursery school, public school, Head Start program, day care center, or
family day care home. Minor modifications for family day care homes
are as follows: Home caregivers are more likely to provide supervisory
support to one another than to receive it from nonprogram administrators; enrollment limits are lower in infant and toddler programs than
in programs for three- to five-year-olds; and developmentally appropriate activities vary with the ages of the youngsters served.

Administrators must keep in mind that it is possible to strive for a
high-quality program even when obstacles prohibit the full realization
of certain components. A kindergarten classroom with 25 or 30 children can nevertheless maintain a child development educational
model based on child-initiated learning activities. We are not advocat-
ing complacency about large class size, but this is not a legitimate ex-
cuse to stop striving for high quality.

A Child Development Educational Model

Each of the components listed in Table 2 is important in the operation
of a high-quality early childhood program, but the most important
component is the **child development educational model.**

Imagine that you have a message to deliver to one of the kindergarten teachers in the school where you are principal. You enter the
kindergarten classroom and do not see either the teacher or the teaching
assistant in the front of the classroom. Gazing around the classroom, you

TABLE 2

COMPONENTS OF HIGH-QUALITY EARLY CHILDHOOD PROGRAMS

A child development educational model

Low enrollment limits, with a teaching/caregiving team assigned to each group of children

Staff trained in early childhood development

Supervisory support and inservice training for a child development educational model

Involvement of parents as partners with program staff

Sensitivity to the noneducational needs of the child and family

Developmentally appropriate evaluation procedures

---

see children busily at work, barely noticing that you came in. They are in the art area, the block area, and the music area—and there's the teacher kneeling on the carpeted floor talking to a boy in the quiet area. There's also a teaching assistant with several children in the house area, trying on dress-up clothes. The teacher notices you and beckons. You walk over and join the teacher in a brief conversation. On your way out, you stop to ask a girl in the art area to tell you about the picture that she is painting.

You have just imagined a scene that presents elements of a good early childhood program. The teachers in such a program recognize children's intellectual, social, and physical needs and encourage them to initiate their own learning activities within a supportive environment that is based on a child development educational model. There are several types of child development educational models—High/Scope (Hohmann & Weikart, 2002), Montessori (1967), and the Creative Curriculum (Dodge, Colker, & Heroman, 2002), for example. While each has its own traditions of development and research, they all embrace certain child development principles.

RECOGNIZING THE VALUE OF CHILD-INITIATED LEARNING ACTIVITY

As U.S. psychologists became involved in early childhood education in the 1960s, they developed early childhood models based on various psychological theories. Some of these models emphasized child-initiated learning activity; others emphasized teacher-directed lessons. Some model developers, including High/Scope founder David Weikart and his colleagues, began to recognize the validity of theories like those of developmental psychologist Jean Piaget. Piaget's concern was with the cognitive development of preschoolers, which he claimed was centered on their thinking about the physical world of toys and objects rather than the symbolic world of reading, writing, and arithmetic. Accordingly, many early childhood educators began to emphasize in their programs children's cognitive development as well as their social-emotional and physical development.

A child development educational model is grounded in Piaget's (1970) persuasive rationale for the learning value of children's intentional learning activity. He held that children learn by actively exploring their environment with all their senses, by thinking about their actions, and by engaging in conversations with each other and with teachers. *There's ample opportunity for children's self-initiated learning activity in a child development educational model, where children have many opportunities to initiate their own activities and take responsibility for completing them; the teacher's role is to help children as they make decisions, not to make all the decisions for them.* The teachers do not rely on workbooks or attempt to maintain strict control. They *are* preparing children for academic learning—not by presenting precisely sequenced lessons of reading, writing, and arithmetic, but by emphasizing children's decision making and problem solving. Such an approach prepares children for the work demands of both the academic and the wider world that they will eventually face.

The core of a child development education model is child-initiated learning activity in which *children choose an activity within a supportive learning framework created by the teacher.* Children then carry out the activity as they choose to do so, not as the teacher directs them to do. Child-initiated learning activity is distinguished from random activity by its purposefulness and from teacher-directed activity by the fact that the child controls what happens. As an example of child-initiated learning activity, consider children electing to paint pictures of their own design. This is not a random activity, nor is it without teacher support, because the teacher has provided the paint, the paper, the space, and the conditions of use as a framework within which children's self-directed activity can occur. Furthermore, as the teacher and children later discuss the paintings, it is the children who describe and explain their work to the teacher, enabling the teacher to label each painting with the child's words and perhaps ask the child to elaborate his or her response by telling a story about the painting that the teacher writes down.

The primary alternative to child-initiated learning activity is the teacher lecture, which is virtually synonymous with formal schooling in the minds of many people. *It is important for administrators to understand that teacher lectures, teacher-centered discussions, and paperwork must be modified and limited for use with young children.*

SOME PRINCIPLES OF CHILD-INITIATED LEARNING ACTIVITY

Drawing on early childhood development theory, research, and practice, we can state several interrelated principles that distinguish child-initiated learning activity:

Child-initiated learning activity acknowledges both the developmental limits of young children and their potential for learning. At one extreme are some educational thinkers who overlook the value of early childhood education, believing that the developmental limits of young children preclude meaningful learning outside their homes. At the other extreme are those who virtually deny any developmental limits of young children, holding that children can learn anything, including reading, writing, and arithmetic, if it is organized in small steps.

The best early childhood learning activities are child-initiated, developmentally appropriate, and open-ended. They are *child-initiated* to take advantage of children's curiosity and motivation to learn from such activities. They are *developmentally appropriate,* meaning they are matched to children's interests and abilities, neither too easy nor too difficult. They are *open-ended* in that they allow for more than one acceptable response or way of acting, a characteristic found more often than not in real-life situations.

Open communication between teacher and child and among children broadens children's perspectives as they learn to share ideas. A long tradition of research on teaching and childrearing has pointed to the superiority of a "democratic" or "authoritative" style of teaching or childrearing that is an alternative to both "authoritarian" and "permissive" styles (Baumrind, 1971). Piaget explained that as children grow up, they learn to take on the perspectives of other people, particularly their peers, if given the opportunity to do so. If they interact mainly with highly authoritarian adults, they will not learn the balanced give-and-take that is essential in much human interaction (Piaget, 1932).

LOW ENROLLMENT LIMITS

It is essential to maintain the favorable staff-child ratio and small group size that are hallmarks of high-quality early childhood programs. Most studies have found that the fewer children per adult, the better the adult and child behavior in early childhood programs (Phillips, 1987). Smaller groups of children experience more constructive adult behavior and achieve more positive developmental outcomes (Phillips, 1987).

In the 1970s, the National Day Care Study found that for 3- to 5-year-olds with 2 adults in the classroom, an enrollment limit of 20 was required for children to merely maintain a normal rate of development of knowledge and skills (Ruopp, Travers, Glantz, & Coelen, 1979, pp. 93–95). Such an enrollment limit therefore seems appropriate to programs for children of average or better than average intellectual ability and socioeconomic circumstances. However, the same study found that an enrollment limit of 16 would be best for a Head Start or state prekindergarten program that serves primarily children who live in poverty or are otherwise at special risk of school failure. (Although High/Scope's successful Perry Preschool program had enrollments of up to 25 poor children, it also had a teaching staff of 4, which is a staff-child ratio of about 1 to 6.) For children below age 3, the National Day Care Study recommended the following: 1 infant per adult; an enrollment limit of 8 children with 2 adults for children from infancy to age 2; and a limit of 12 children with 3 adults for 2-year-olds (Ruopp et al., 1979, pp. 158–160).

What does this mean for those of us who have enrollments well above the recommended levels? Elementary school principals often find themselves in a position in which the enrollment limits of their kindergarten programs and even prekindergarten programs substantially exceed the limits recommended here. The U.S. public elementary school pupil-teacher ratio was 16.7 children per teacher in 1999 (National Center for Education Statistics, 2001), meaning that about half of the nation's elementary classrooms had more pupils than that.

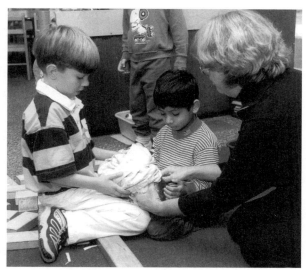

The way adults and children communicate says a lot about the quality of an early childhood program.

In such circumstances, we should still encourage our teachers to emphasize child-initiated, developmentally appropriate learning activities, even though it is a more difficult task; staff will need strong administrative support. You might encourage them to invite parents to assist them in the classroom. There may be older students or senior citizens in the community who could offer classroom support. Such volunteers need supervisory support, but their contributions can be substantial. Together with the school district administration, you must decide whether your early childhood programs are operating with adequate funding, and if they are not, you should take a course of action to move towards that goal.

TRAINED STAFF

Adults who provide care and education for young children need specialized training in child development and early childhood education (Ceglowski & Bacigalupa, 2002; Phillips, 1987). One study found that such training leads teachers to be less authoritarian and punitive and to have a more positive interaction style (Arnett, 1989). Adults' general level of education has also been associated with program quality and effectiveness (Howes, 1997; Whitebook, Howes, & Phillips, 1998).

The care and education of young children is a legitimate teaching specialization. Familiarity with teaching children in the upper elementary grades does not qualify a teacher to work with three- to five-year-olds; in fact, such experience or training may even be a hindrance if the teacher does not have a nurturing, nondirective teaching style and does not develop a set of expectations appropriate to younger children. If you must ask teachers who are untrained in early childhood to teach in prekindergarten or kindergarten classrooms, you should encourage and help them to obtain early childhood training as soon as possible.

In the long term, however, *it is important that you employ well-trained staff who are certified to teach in programs for young children.* Some states recognize the need for this type of staff training, and this may help your cause; 18 states required a bachelor's degree for prekindergarten teachers in 2002 (Education Commission of the States, 2002). In general, to be certified, a teacher must have a bachelor's degree with a major area of specialization, such as early childhood. Another approach to early childhood teacher certification is the competency-based Child Development Associate credential now administered by the Council for Early Childhood Professional Recognition.

Persons who argue against requiring such credentials or other evidence of early childhood training may claim that anybody can take care of young children; however, such a claim is not consistent with research findings. Nor does it recognize the special teaching/caregiving style required to work successfully with groups of young children—a skill that incorporates and goes beyond parenting skill. True, some people are naturally gifted with this style, but most of us must develop it through training and experience. It is also true that adults without early childhood credentials can contribute constructively to early childhood programs, but they must be well supervised and must receive inservice training.

Another important point related to the professionalism and training of early childhood educators concerns salaries. Once teachers and caregivers are adequately trained, they have achieved professional status and should receive salaries that reflect this professionalism. To attract talent-

Preschool staff must be adequately trained in child development and early childhood education and adequately compensated.

ed young people to the early childhood profession, it seems reasonable to offer them salaries on a par with those of elementary school teachers. Yet, in 2000, preschool teachers earned $20,100, a level comparable to that of janitors and hairdressers and only half that of kindergarten teachers ($40,230; Bureau of Labor Statistics, 2002a). Fortunately, despite these low salaries, some preschool teachers are highly educated and experienced and very good at their jobs. Whether they work in schools, child care centers, or child care homes, they are the primary resource for expertise in operating your early childhood programs.

SUPERVISORY SUPPORT AND INSERVICE TRAINING

As an administrator, you should understand and actively support the goals and operation of an early childhood program and its curriculum. Be prepared to do the following:

- Explain and defend your educational model to parents, other teachers and staff, other administrators, and community leaders

- Be sure that staff, children, and the program itself are evaluated by developmentally appropriate measures and standards

- Provide the program with the equipment and resources necessary for a developmentally appropriate educational model

- Hire qualified staff, see that they receive adequate compensation, and encourage teamwork among staff in each classroom

- Enable staff to spend at least 30 minutes a day in program planning

- Allocate staff time for monthly inservice training sessions and assure that these sessions lead to systematic application of child development principles in the classroom

- Work with staff and parents to resolve parents' before- and after-school child care needs

Administrators are especially responsible for the **inservice training** of early childhood staff. Such training ought to take place at least monthly to address issues that arise in the program's day-to-day operation, particularly those centering on the educational model used. When you provide good inservice training, you give your staff the opportunity to increase their professionalism and to receive encouragement and emotional support from other teachers (as well as from you) in their efforts to implement the educational model. Some building principals and program directors can take advantage of the inservice training opportunities provided by their district's or agency's early childhood specialist. If you do not have such opportunities, you can encourage your early childhood staff to form study groups in which they read and discuss early childhood materials, such as articles in *Young Children,* the journal of the National Association for the Education of Young Children. In addition, you can send your staff to various early childhood conferences and/or education programs at local universities, where they will associate with other early childhood educators and stay current with the most recent developments in the early childhood field. (To help you in such efforts, we have included a list of national information sources on early childhood programs in Appendix B.)

PARENT INVOLVEMENT

We know that parent involvement is essential to good education programs throughout children's schooling, but it is difficult to develop effective parent outreach programs, particularly when so many parents are in the workforce. There are no easy solutions to this problem. Nevertheless, achieving successful parent involvement is especially important in high-quality early childhood programs and therefore requires creative thinking about how to overcome the obstacles encountered.

A high-quality early childhood program involves parents and is sensitive to their needs. Recognizing parents' crucial importance in children's development, you and your staff need to form a partnership with them. Being partners means that you and your staff should be able to explain child development principles to parents. Being partners also means that if parents want to help their 4-year-old learn to read, you can show them how to focus on the emerging language and literacy skills, such as learning letter sounds and vocabulary, that are most appropriate for children at this age.

Being partners means neither being too authoritarian towards parents (for example, claiming to know what's best for the child regardless of parental perceptions) nor being too accommodating to them when they want inappropriate academic demands placed on young children. Being partners means you and your teachers are the recognized experts on principles of child development and should be acknowledged as such by parents, but parents are the long-standing experts on their children's behavior, traits, and family background. When you can help parents see their children's usual behavior in developmental terms, you and your staff provide a valuable service.

Being partners with parents means you and your early childhood staff help them develop appropriate expectations for their young children. Some parents hold unnecessarily low expectations for their children; they do not recognize the potential value of early childhood education in helping their children achieve developmentally appropriate knowledge, skills, and positive attitudes. Other parents have expectations that are too high and demanding. Parents at any socioeconomic level may hold inappropriate expectations for children, either too low or too high. You and your staff have the opportunity to help these parents. For example, if parents drop off and pick up their child at school, your teaching teams can seize this opportunity to talk with them about their child's progress. Your staff should also meet with parents, individually or as a group, at least monthly to discuss program-related topics. In some cases, staff may have to reach uninvolved parents by scheduling home visits. Because most parents are eager to learn more about their child's development and progress, you could offer discussions at parent meetings on how to discipline children properly, how to support and encourage child-initiated learning activities, how to engage in parent-child activities that promote development, and how to assess a child's developmental status and progress. Your active participation in parent-staff meetings can contribute greatly to their success.

Being partners with parents means encouraging them to come into the classroom. Parents can achieve greater understanding of and sensitivity to child development by joining the teaching/caregiving team in the classroom as well as in daily planning sessions. Parents should be encouraged to participate in the classroom *in a meaningful capacity*—either as informed observers or as volunteer assistants who provide teaching and care.

SENSITIVITY TO THE NONEDUCATIONAL NEEDS OF CHILDREN AND FAMILIES

In addition to wanting to know how to help their young children develop in age-appropriate ways, families wrestle with many other challenges. Consider, for example, that nearly three-fourths of all mothers are in the labor force: 79% of mothers whose youngest child is 6 to 17, 72% of mothers whose youngest child is 3 to 5 years old, and 61% of mothers whose youngest child is under 3 years old (Bureau of Labor Statistics, 2002b). Children with employed parents need *child care arrangements* for the parents' full work day, whenever it might be. If they are in a school-based early childhood program that operates either part-day or for the full school day, they need child care arrangements for the remainder of the work day. Of all children under 5 years old, 63% have a regular child care arrangement. Of these children, 65% receive care from a family member or other relative, either in the child's home or in the relative's home. Nonrelatives in private homes provide care to 28%, and day care centers, nursery schools, and Head Start take care of 32% (Smith, 2002).

For these reasons it would be helpful for you and your staff to get to know the child care providers of the children in your school. These may be providers who operate day care centers or day care homes or who participate in less formal arrangements. A primary point of contact for school staff and child care providers is in the arranging of transportation for the children. School buses can provide transportation between the school and the child care facility. The public school can serve as a convenient site for meetings of the community's early childhood teachers and caregivers.

When both parents in a family are employed, parent-staff communication is difficult to schedule and must be pursued vigorously. Encourage your staff to schedule evening conferences, possibly in parents' homes, to accommodate the schedules of working parents. This problem involves the business community as well as parents and teachers. The Committee for Economic Development (1985) once recommended that "business develop flexible policies that allow and encourage both parents and interested nonparents, especially those who are hourly employees, to participate actively in the community's schools" (p. 26). Such a recommendation should be applied as well to prekindergarten programs that are not in schools. Try to work out cooperative arrangements with local businesses that would provide release time for parents to attend school functions or to serve as volunteers in classrooms.

Consider also the issue of child and family poverty. The poverty rate among children under age 6 was 18% in 2001 (Proctor & Dalaker, 2002). Fortunately, this rate has steadily declined from its high point of 26% in 1993, but it is still well above its modern low point of 15% in 1969 (Bureau of the Census, 2002). Since it began operation in 1965, the national Head Start program has focused primarily on children living in poverty. Forty-three states currently fund early learning programs for young children prior to kindergarten, and most of these programs are aimed at children who are living in poverty or are otherwise at risk of school failure (Education Commission of the States, 2000).

Experience has shown that if an education program for impoverished children is to make sense, the basic needs of the children and their families must be addressed. Children need adequate nutrition, and young children living in poverty may well need meals to be provided at the early childhood program site. Also, poor families may need assistance in finding agencies and services to help them. Parents who are poor often lack education and may be unable to read and write in English. Literacy training for parents can go hand in hand with early childhood programs. An evaluation of Kentucky's Parent and Child Education program (PACE) found that the program led 49% of participating parents to complete their high school equivalency certification (GED). In a comparable control group in adult basic education only, only 15% attained the GED (Kim, 1987).

Although you cannot be all things to all people, you and your staff are in a unique position that enables you to offer referrals and to serve as counselors and friends to children and families who live in poverty or who experience other social problems.

Developmentally Appropriate Evaluation Procedures

The two main objectives of early childhood evaluation are to assess program quality and to assess children's development. Your early childhood teachers make decisions about children, and as an administrator, you make decisions about both children and teachers, decisions that are based on either formal or informal evaluations of teachers' and children's behavior and activities. Formal evaluation procedures, by making explicit the criteria for decisions, can make decisions more fair (Puckett & Black, 1999; Spodek & Saracho, 1996).

Assessing Program Quality

Program quality is assessed by comparing what is observed in an early childhood program to a set of standards for quality. To assist you in assessing the quality of your program, we have constructed a simple **early childhood program quality questionnaire** (presented in Figure 1 on p. 28).

Other general program-rating instruments are the Early Childhood Environment Rating Scale (Harms, Clifford, & Cryer, 1998), the NAEYC

Systematic observation of children in classrooms is a valid way to assess their development.

standards of program quality (National Association for the Education of Young Children, 1998), and High/Scope's Preschool Program Quality Assessment (High/Scope Educational Research Foundation, 2003b). The latter instrument, for example, focuses attention on learning environment, daily routine, teacher-child interaction, curriculum planning and assessment, parent involvement and family services, staff qualifications and staff development, and program management.

ASSESSING CHILDREN'S DEVELOPMENT

Systematic observation of children in classrooms, ratings by teachers, and tests are three ways to assess children's development. The various types of tests for young children include tests that screen children for potential educational problems, tests that diagnose the nature of these problems, tests that measure children's school readiness, and tests of curriculum outcomes.

Any test or other assessment method that is used should meet the established criteria for validity and reliability (American Educational

Figure 1
Early Childhood Program Quality Questionnaire

A. Enrollment and Staffing

1. How many children are enrolled in each early childhood classroom in your school?
2. Given the number of teaching staff assigned to these classrooms, what is the teacher-child ratio?
3. How many early childhood teaching staff members are at each of these levels of child development/early childhood education training?

    ____ Master's/doctorate in early childhood development/education
    ____ Bachelor's degree in early childhood development/education
    ____ Child Development Associate credential
    ____ Some college courses in early childhood development/education
    ____ No training in early childhood development/education

B. Supervisory Support and Inservice Training

4. How many minutes a day, week, or month do you spend discussing the educational model and program operation with your early childhood teaching staff?
5. How many minutes a day, week, or month does your early childhood teaching staff have for team planning when they are on the job but not in contact with children?
6. How many hours of inservice training did your early childhood teaching staff have last school year?
7. What were the three most recent inservice-training topics?

C. Parent Involvement

8. How many minutes a day, week, or month does your early childhood teaching staff spend with parents in informal discussions about children?
9. How many meetings with parent groups did your early childhood teaching staff hold during the last school year?
10. What were the topics of the last three of these meetings?
11. How many meetings with individual parents, at school or in their homes, did your early childhood teaching staff have during the last school year?

D. Noneducational Needs of Children and Families

12. Does your early childhood teaching staff know what other early childhood care education arrangements their children have?
13. Did your staff meet during the last school year with these other teachers and day care providers?
14. Does your early childhood teaching staff know how to make referrals to social agencies for families who live in poverty or face other problems?
15. Does your early childhood teaching staff recognize children's handicaps and know how to make appropriate referrals?

E.   Child Development Educational Model

16. Are the early childhood classrooms arranged in interest areas?
17. Do the early childhood classrooms have a balance of materials, commercial and noncommercial, that are accessible to the children and that have a variety of uses?
18. Do children in the early childhood classrooms spend a substantial portion of time each day in activities that they initiate themselves with teacher support?
19. In group activities, are the children given opportunities to make choices about activities?
20. Does your early childhood teaching staff spend substantial time talking to children as individuals and in small groups?

Research Association, American Psychological Association, & National Council of Measurement in Education, 1999). In the assessment of young children's performance, two aspects of validity have special importance—developmental validity and predictive validity. **Developmental validity** means that the performance items being measured are developmentally suitable for the children being assessed. At the early childhood level (ages 3 to 7), performance items should represent what Piaget called preoperational thinking. This includes such intellectual skills as placing things in categories and ranking them by some physical attribute. **Predictive validity** means that an early childhood measure can predict children's later school success or failure, as defined by achievement test scores or academic placements (that is, on-grade, retained in grade, or placed in special education) during the elementary grades. Over the longer term, predictive validity can even refer to such potential outcomes of the educational process as literacy, employment, or avoiding criminal activity.

Sometimes, assessment measures are used to screen children for program entry. If an early childhood program is not open to all children of a certain age, children must be selected for the program by some criteria. These criteria generally focus in some way on risk of school failure.

Unfortunately, valid and reliable screening tests are virtually non-existent for children under 3 years of age, and only a handful exist for 3- to 6-year-olds. One review of screening instruments recommended only four of the many that are on the market—the Denver Developmental Screening Test, the Early Screening Inventory, the McCarthy

Screening Test, and the Minneapolis Preschool Screening Instrument (Meisels, 1994). Not all options involve tests, however. For example, one option is to select for program entry children living in poverty, clearly a major impediment to school success. Another option is to select children on the basis of some screening test that identifies them as being at risk of school failure. A third option is to use some combination of the poverty criterion and the screening-test criterion.

Group-administered academic achievement tests are inappropriate for preschool-aged children in content, format, and the sustained attention that they require of children. Such tests assume test-taking skills that preschool-aged children have not yet developed. Early childhood education does not speed up children's academic achievement; rather, it builds a solid foundation for it. Individual testing is possible, but should be complemented by observational assessment.

High/Scope's **Preschool Child Observation Record** (2003a) is an example of a developmentally valid observational instrument. (An infant-toddler version is also available [High/Scope Educational Research Foundation, 2002].) It relies on systematic classroom observations of young children's performance by trained teachers or observers. It is based on a series of written records of children's performance over the course of several weeks or months. Child Observation Record items represent the domains of language and literacy, logic and mathematics, creative representation, music and movement, social relations, and initiative. A study of COR ratings of children's behavior by 64 teams of COR-trained Head Start teachers and assistant teachers demonstrated the COR's reliability and concurrent validity.

Now that we have reviewed the hallmarks of a high-quality early childhood program, let's take a closer look at the child development education model developed and validated by the High/Scope Educational Research Foundation.

3

THE HIGH/SCOPE EDUCATIONAL MODEL

Since child-initiated learning activity is essential to early childhood education and has such widespread appeal in the early childhood field, many formal and informal early childhood educational models now embrace it. Child-initiated learning activity, as we have defined it, is central to the models espoused by such early childhood education schools and training facilities as Bank Street College of Education in New York City; the Erikson Institute in Chicago; Pacific Oaks College in Pasadena, California; Teaching Strategies, Inc. in Washington, DC; and the High/Scope Educational Research Foundation in Ypsilanti, Michigan. It has similar status in the educational ideas and practices advocated by the early childhood departments of most U.S. colleges and universities and by the Child Development Associate training conducted by the Council for Early Childhood Professional Recognition.

But some early childhood educational models do not emphasize all aspects of child-initiated learning activity. A basic tenet regarding such activity is that it should include open-ended communication between teachers and children that can broaden the children's perspective as they learn to share ideas that are not first presented by the teacher. This type of interaction acknowledges both the developmental limits of young children and their vast potential for learning; thus, the resultant learning activities are *developmentally appropriate*. In developmentally appropriate learning programs, young children engage in purposeful learning and make decisions about their activities. With this focus to guide us, we will describe the High/Scope educational model, one of various developmentally appropriate educational models.

The High/Scope educational model is a coordinated set of ideas and practices in early childhood education originally formulated in the 1960s by the staff of the High/Scope Educational Research Foundation, under the leadership of David P. Weikart (Hohmann & Weikart, 2002; Weikart & Schweinhart, 1999). Today, the High/Scope model is being systematically employed in over 13,000 classrooms throughout the U.S. and in many other countries (Epstein, 1993).

The fundamental premise of the High/Scope model, which is based on the child development ideas of Jean Piaget, is that children learn best from activities that they plan and carry out themselves. Teachers and children work together with mutual respect. The teachers arrange interest areas in the classroom and maintain a daily routine that permits children to plan and carry out their own activities, as well as participate in group activities. During these activities, the teachers join in and ask children questions that help them think. The teachers keep in mind and encourage various **key experiences** that help children learn to talk with others about personally meaningful experiences, express feelings in words, sort and match objects, move with objects, and engage in other actions that promote healthy intellectual, social, and physical development.

Unlike many other educational models, the High/Scope model does not require the purchase of special materials; the only cost involved is that of equipping the classroom in a way typical of any good nursery school program. While the initial changeover to High/Scope methodology may be challenging for some teachers, once mastered, this methodology frees them for comfortable work with children, other teachers, and supervisors. The High/Scope model has worked well with children in many countries over the years. It is firmly linked to both developmental theory and historical practice, and it has been validated through longitudinal studies over the past 40 years. Further, it lends itself to teacher training and supervision, so that parents and administrators can rest assured that high-quality programs are being provided for children.

Learning Activities Planned by the Child

The critical principle underlying the High/Scope model is that teachers must be fully committed to providing settings in which children participate in planning their own learning activities and constructing their own knowledge. The child's knowledge comes from personal interaction with the world—from direct experience with real objects and the application of logical thinking to this experience, along with the input of cultural information. The teacher's role is to encourage these experiences through a suitable classroom arrangement and supportive questioning style that helps the child think about these experiences logically. In a sense, children are expected to learn by the scientific method of observation and inference, at a level of complexity that fits their development. The essence of the scientific method is learning from experience, and even the youngest child does that.

ROLE OF THE TEACHER

Children and teachers alike join in planning learning activities in the High/Scope educational model. By their own daily evaluation and planning, teachers analyze their experiences with children and consider classroom activities that occurred that day. In this way, teachers strive to

The High/Scope Educational Model is being implemented in thousands of U.S. classrooms and in many foreign countries.

achieve new insights into each child's unique blend of skills and interests. Teachers strive to challenge themselves by observing one another's performance and interacting with fellow staff in mutually supportive ways.

An important aspect of the High/Scope model is the guiding role of teachers. While broad developmental milestones are employed to monitor children's progress, teachers do not plan every aspect of every activity. Instead, they listen closely to what children plan and then work with them to extend their activities to challenging levels. The questioning style teachers use is one that elicits information from the child—information that can help a teacher participate in the activity or that can lead to the child's further activity. They rarely use testlike questions about color, number, or size; instead, they ask, What has happened? How can you make what you want? Show me what you mean. Can you help your classmate? Such a supportive questioning style permits free conversation between teacher and child. It also serves as model language for children to use with one another. This approach permits teachers and children to interact as cooperative thinkers and doers rather than as dominant teachers and passive pupils. All are sharing and learning as they work.

The High/Scope model shares with historic early childhood approaches, such as those of Froebel and Montessori, an emphasis on the child as an active learner. It differs from these approaches, however, in that it uses cognitive-developmental theory to place primary emphasis on problem solving and independent thinking, while the older approaches have focused on social development and relationships. In the High/Scope model, teachers continuously gauge the child's developmental status and present intellectual challenges intended to stretch the child's awareness and understanding. In social-development approaches, the child's active learning takes place because the teacher stands out of the way and permits it to take place, not because the teacher encourages it to happen. In some Montessori programs, for example, teachers view themselves as guests in the child's classroom environment.

A DAILY ROUTINE TO SUPPORT CHILDREN'S PLANNING OF LEARNING ACTIVITIES

To create a setting in which children join in planning their own learning activities, teachers maintain a consistent daily classroom routine that varies only when the child has fair warning that things will be different the next day. They do not change the daily routine without good reason and advance notice to the children. This adherence to routine provides a learning environment that enables children to enjoy the opportunity to make independent decisions and to develop a sense of responsibility for their actions.

The daily routine in the High/Scope model is made up of a **plan-do-review** sequence, group times, and several additional elements. The plan-do-review sequence is the central device in the model that gives children opportunities to make choices about their activities and yet keeps the teacher intimately involved in the whole process. The elements of the daily routine are described in the following paragraphs.

Planning time. Children make choices and decisions all the time, but they are not usually encouraged to think about these decisions in a systematic way or to realize the possibilities and consequences related to the choices they have made. During planning time, children have the opportunity to express their ideas to teachers and to see themselves as individuals who can act on decisions. They experience the power of independence and the joy of working with an attentive teacher as well as with peers.

The teacher and child together discuss the child's plans before they are carried out. This helps children form mental pictures of their ideas and obtain notions about how to proceed. For teachers, developing a plan with the child provides not only an opportunity to encourage and respond to the child's ideas and to make suggestions to assure the plan's success, but also a chance to understand and gauge the child's unique level of development and thinking style. Both children and teachers receive benefits: children feel supported and ready to start their plans, while teachers have ideas of what to look for, what difficulties children might have, and where help might be needed. In such a classroom both children and teachers assume appropriate roles of equal importance.

Work time. The "do" part of the plan-do-review sequence is work time, the period after children have finished planning. It is generally the longest single time period in the daily routine and is a busy and active period for both the children and teachers.

Teachers new to this model sometimes find work time confusing because they are not sure of their role. Teachers do not lead work-time activities—children execute their own plans of work—but neither do

Children follow their own interests during work time—the "do" part of the plan-do-review sequence.

teachers just sit back and passively watch. The teacher's role during work time is first to *observe* children to see how they are learning, interacting with peers, and solving problems, and then to *enter into the children's activities* to encourage, extend, and set up problem-solving situations.

Clean-up time. Clean-up time is wedged into the plan-do-review sequence in the obvious place, after the "doing." During this time, children return materials and equipment to their places and store their incomplete projects. This process not only restores order to the classroom but provides opportunities for children to assume responsibility for restoring order as they sort materials and put them away.

The way the classroom is organized is of special importance. All materials in the classroom that are intended for children's use are within their reach and on open shelves. Clear labeling and ordering are essential, usually with pictures or simple drawings and printed labels pinpointing where children are to store the objects on the shelf.

With such an organizational plan, children can realistically return all work materials to their appropriate places and use many basic cognitive skills in doing so.

Recall time. Recall time is the final phase of the plan-do-review sequence. The children represent their work-time experiences in a variety of ways appropriate to their developmental levels. They might recall the names of the children they involved in their plan, draw a picture of the building they made, or recount the problems they encountered. Recall strategies include children drawing pictures of what they did, making models, reviewing their plans, or verbally recalling the past events. Recall time brings closure to children's planning and work time activities. Part of the teacher's role is to help children realize the connection between their actual work and their original plan.

Small-group time. The format of small-group time is familiar to all preschool teachers: The teacher presents an activity in which children participate for a set period of time. These activities are drawn from the cultural background of the children, from field trips the group has taken, from the seasons of the year, and from other age-appropriate group activities involving cooking, art, music and movement, and so on. Although teachers structure the activity, children are encouraged to contribute ideas and solve in their own way problems presented by the teacher. Activities follow no prescribed sequence, but respond to the children's needs, abilities, interests, and cognitive goals. Once children have had the opportunity to make personal choices and solve problems, the teacher can further extend the children's ideas and actions by asking them open-ended questions or setting up additional problem-solving situations.

An active small-group time such as those described here gives children valuable learning experiences, including opportunities to explore materials and objects, use their senses, make choices and decisions, solve problems, and work with teachers and other children.

Large-group/circle time. At circle time, the whole group meets together with a teacher for 10 to 15 minutes to play games, sing songs, do finger plays, do basic movement exercises, play musical instruments, or re-enact a special event. Circle time provides an opportunity for each child to participate in a large group, share and demonstrate ideas, and learn from the ideas of others.

Key Experiences in Child Development

In the High/Scope model, teachers review children's progress by using a set of **key experiences.** Just as the plan-do-review sequence conducted with a consistent daily routine is the process of the High/Scope model, so are the key experiences the content. Key experiences are a way of helping the teacher support and extend the child's self-designed activity so that developmentally appropriate experiences and opportunities for growth are constantly available to the child. They provide a way of thinking about curriculum that frees the teacher from the activity workbooks that characterize some early childhood programs or the scope-and-sequence charts that dominate the behavioral approaches.

The key experiences are important to the growth of rational thought in all young children, regardless of nation or culture. They are also very simple and pragmatic. The domains of key experiences identified thus far are the following:

- Creative representation
- Language and literacy
- Initiative and social relations
- Movement
- Music
- Classification
- Seriation
- Number
- Space
- Time

These domains are further divided into types of experiences. For example, the language and literacy domain has the following types of key experiences:

- Talking with others about personally meaningful experiences
- Describing objects, events, and relations
- Having fun with language: listening to stories and poems, making up stories and rhymes

- Writing in various ways: drawing, scribbling, making letterlike forms, invented spelling, conventional forms
- Reading in various ways: reading storybooks, signs and symbols, one's own writing
- Dictating stories

Initiative and Social Relations has the following subdivisions:

- Making and expressing choices, plans, and decisions
- Solving problems encountered in play
- Taking care of one's own needs
- Expressing feelings in words
- Participating in group routines
- Being sensitive to the feelings, interests, and needs of others
- Building relationships with children and adults
- Creating and experiencing collaborative play
- Dealing with social conflict

The key experiences are not mutually exclusive, and any given learning activity may involve more than one type of experience. Yet this approach gives the teacher a clear frame of reference in thinking about the program and the youngsters. In addition, the key-experience approach provides structure to the curriculum while allowing room for new types of experiences. Thus, as High/Scope staff develop the educational model in the various domains, they will identify additional key experiences. The key experiences concept assures that the High/Scope model will continue to expand its potential contribution to children's healthy growth and development.

Throughout this discussion of the educational model, we have indicated its flexibility in various ways. The model is an educational model because it is both an instructional model that defines teaching practices and a content model that identifies learning outcomes for children through its key experiences. But in both respects, it is an open model that can accommodate new practices and new sets of outcomes for children, as long as they are consistent with its basic orientation.

Role of Parents and Community

From the outset of development of the High/Scope model, parent participation has been important. In the initial period, teachers made home visits each week to each participating family, with the focus usually on the mother and participating child. The key to effective parent involvement is recognition of the interrelated roles of parents and teachers: While school staff have valuable knowledge to impart to the family about their child's development and the educational model that is in use, parents have equally important information to impart to the school staff about the child's family culture, language, and goals. The recognition that parents and staff are both experts in their own domains is essential to the success of the program.

Training in the High/Scope Educational Model

Effective training in the High/Scope model has certain key elements. Training is **model-focused** and usually **on-site.** It must be **adapted to the actual work setting of the teacher** (to the equipment, space, and so on) and **adapted to the group of children involved** (for example, children with disabilities or children for whom English is a second language). It must also be **related to the culture of the children,** in order to involve parents in some systematic way.

Training sessions are ideally scheduled about once a month, because teachers need a period of time to put training into practice, share it, think about it, see the gaps in their own thinking, see the gaps in the program being presented, and make adaptations to their own setting. Each teacher should experience consistent delivery of training, supported by consistent observation and feedback. High/Scope staff and certified trainers around the world are helping to provide the support necessary to establish and maintain high-quality programs with adequately trained teachers.

In the final chapter, we turn to an examination of the school readiness movement today—the new emphasis on what children learn from their experiences in early childhood programs.

4

THE SCHOOL READINESS MOVEMENT TODAY

The school readiness movement is the most important development affecting early childhood programs since this booklet was first published in 1988. This last chapter describes this movement and how it affects early childhood programs and their relationship with schools.

In February 1990, the U.S. president and the 50 state governors adopted national education goals. The first goal was that by the year 2000, all children would start school ready to learn (National Education Goals Panel, 2002). Even though this goal was not fully achieved by the designated time, it moved school readiness to center stage in early childhood education. Previously, school readiness was of central concern only to the Gesell Institute and a few others, while other educators had little use for it. Its adoption as a national education goal by the nation's political leaders gave it an unprecedented priority in the thinking of the nation's educators. As more educators fit it into their thinking, they defined it according to their own educational ideas, and it continues to have various shades of meaning.

The National Education Goals Panel itself (1991) elaborated the readiness goal into three objectives relating to what children need to be ready for school:

- "Children will receive the nutrition, physical activity experiences, and health care needed to arrive at school with healthy minds and bodies, and to maintain the mental alertness necessary to be prepared to learn, and the number of low-birth-weight babies will be significantly reduced through enhanced prenatal health systems."

- "Every parent in the United States will be a child's first teacher and devote time each day to helping such parent's preschool child learn, and parents will have access to the training and support parents need."

- "All children will have access to high-quality and developmentally appropriate preschool programs that help prepare children for school."

The Goal One Resource and Technical Planning Group (1993) suggested that school readiness has five dimensions:

1. **Physical well-being and motor development** includes physical development, physical abilities, and background and contextual factors.

2. **Social and emotional development** involves the individual's interactions with peers and adults and feeling states regarding the self and others.

3. **Approaches toward learning** comprises children's predispositions influenced by gender, temperament, and culture; and learning styles, such as curiosity, initiative, task persistence, attentiveness, imagination, and cognitive styles.

4. **Language development** includes the verbal language abilities to listen, speak, use language in context, use vocabulary, question, and be creative with language; the emerging literacy abilities of being aware of letter sounds, print, and literature; and understanding a story and writing.

5. **Cognition and general knowledge** involves physical knowledge of objects in external reality; logico-mathematical knowledge of the relationships created by individuals within their minds between objects, events, and people, such as similarities, differences, and associations; and social-conventional knowledge of the agreed-upon conventions of society and school-learned knowledge that cannot be reinvented by learners.

The readiness goal was one of the first recognitions of a growing demand that early childhood programs demonstrate their contribution to children's development and readiness for school. Congress voiced this same demand in the 1998 reauthorization of the federal Head Start program (U.S. Congress, 1998) by calling for all Head Start agencies to assess children's development. The Head Start Bureau (2000) subsequently developed a Head Start Child Outcomes Framework that features indicators in eight domain areas—language development, literacy, mathematics, science, creative arts, social and emotional development, approaches toward learning, and physical health and development. Both the Goals Panel definition and the Head Start framework are comprehensive, encompassing not only the traditional school domains of literacy and mathematics but also the various other domains of cognitive, social, and physical development. Head Start will continue to develop its effort to assess children's development, both to help teaching staff improve their programs and to hold the programs accountable for delivering on their great promise.

The National Education Goals Panel took seriously the idea that just as children should be ready for school, so should schools be ready for children. In so doing, it developed a list of key characteristics of ready schools that can serve as guidelines for elementary school administrators. The Goal 1 Ready Schools Resource Group (Shore, 1998) identified the following key characteristics of ready schools:

1. **Ready schools smooth the transition between home and school.** The report says that ready schools pay attention to the transitions that children and their parents make as they move from the familiar home setting and from preschool or child care to the kindergarten classroom. They work closely with parents and community organizations; get to know children in the settings they live in; bring children's daily experience into the classroom; and celebrate the oral traditions of children's communities. They send welcoming letters or make home visits and hold orientation sessions for children and parents before the children begin school. They invite fathers and other family members as well as mothers and allow plenty of time for questions and answers.

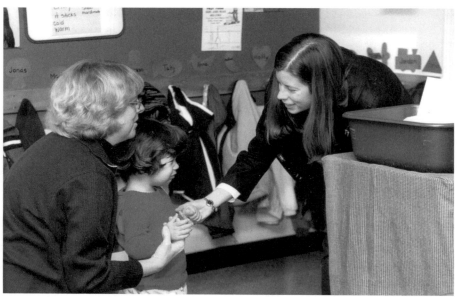

Ready schools help parents and children make smooth transitions between home and the classroom.

The first day of school in a ready school is a special day. Principal and teachers meet and greet children and parents at the door and endeavor to make the children feel secure, happy, and capable of success in this new setting. Ready schools help parents get their children ready for kindergarten. They encourage them to read to their young children, take parent education courses, take their children for regular doctor visits and immunizations, find high-quality early childhood programs, get early assistance for children with disabilities, and finish school if they have not done so.

2. **Ready schools strive for continuity between early care and education programs and elementary schools.** The report notes that most young children experience some type of out-of-home care, and most 3- to 5-year-olds participate in some type of preschool program. Thus, they ought to experience continuity in classroom climate and educational model from these programs to kindergarten, but in fact many kindergartens have

become narrowly focused on academic goals, making children's transition more difficult. If preschool and kindergarten teachers communicate with each other and draw on the best practices in both settings, these differences will lessen. Yet a national survey indicates that communication across settings continues to be minimal (Love, Logue, Trudeau, & Thayer, 1992). Good first steps would be for schools to identify their early childhood feeder programs and hold meetings to discuss what to do about children's transition, with designated lead people made responsible for following through.

3. **Ready schools help children learn and make sense of their complex and exciting world.** Ready schools help children to develop literacy, mathematics, and other skills, and to use their knowledge to make sense of the world. A ready school consistently uses an educational model that has been shown to contribute to children's achievement of high standards.

Ready schools provide a high level of quality in their instruction. Instructional techniques make sense to students so that they are consistently engaged in learning. Lessons are clear and meaningful to students, with frequent formal and informal checks to see that they are learning, along with feedback to students. The material is often new to them but always within their reach, and they receive the support of teachers and peers, perhaps through cross-age or peer tutoring. Schools must teach what they want children to know.

Children in ready schools are motivated to pay attention, study, and learn by their use of interesting materials and by frequent encouragement and feedback. Teachers relate materials to children's knowledge and interests and actively involve them in using new skills and knowledge. They let children know they are confident in their ability to learn.

Children in ready schools spend most of their time engaged in purposeful activities that support their learning. Their teachers use good classroom management techniques that avoid wasted time. Subject matter is appropriately rigorous and may be fit into children's work on projects. The curriculum is not fragmented. Children's curiosity is often roused, and they construct knowledge of the world and learn skills through social interaction. Human relationships are central to all learning in a ready school, with collaborative work, work in small groups, and peer coaching as well as whole-group instruction and individual work. Teachers form strong bonds with children, despite any cultural or other differences between them.

4. **Ready schools are committed to the success of every child.** Ready schools are demanding but flexible to meet children's needs. Their curricula and teaching practices are ready, open, and engaging for children. The school's staff is well qualified and knowledgeable. Tutors or other forms of individual attention may be available to children with problems; specialists, such as nurses, computer specialists, and librarians play important roles. The physical facility is safe, appropriate for children's levels of development, and full of stimulating, varied materials. A ready school is clean and well maintained, has plenty of visual displays, and its classrooms are attractive learning environments, with chairs for adults as well as children. Schools, or groupings within them, should be small enough that children, teachers, and other staff know each other's names.

Staff in ready schools go out of their way to bridge cultural gulfs between themselves and children from racial and ethnic minorities and/or low-income families, and to keep children from giving up on school. Teachers have the same expectations for children regardless of their background and give them the help they need to achieve these expectations.

Ready schools have high expectations for children with disabilities and ensure that all children who are eligible have access to special education services. The Individuals with Disabilities Education Act (U.S. Congress, 1997) requires placement of children with disabilities in the least restrictive appro-

Ready schools recognize that teachers are the most important ingredient in school success and are committed to their success.

priate setting—usually a regular classroom, perhaps modified to include them. Individualized Educational Programs for children with disabilities may prescribe for them special services in instruction, curricula, materials, and therapies.

In ready schools, all teachers have the professional development and support they need to meet the needs of all the children in their classrooms. The growing number of language-minority children must receive help to understand the curriculum. Ready schools pay attention to parents' preferences, respect their cultures, and help language-minority children learn in both their languages.

5. **Ready schools are committed to the success of every teacher and every adult who interacts with children during the school day.** Teachers are the most important ingredient in school success. The National Board of Professional Teaching Standards has developed standards for accomplished teachers, including early childhood teachers, and teachers and staff in ready schools engage in ongoing, effective professional development. School leaders can give teachers opportunities and support for professional development and their own academic study, support teacher mentoring programs, and encourage collaborations among teachers. When included in a ready school's professional development activities, preschool teach-

ers can learn about content from elementary school teachers, and elementary school teachers can learn about child-initiated learning from preschool teachers. Both can profit from more opportunities to learn and practice strategies for working with the diverse children they encounter, especially children with disabilities and language-minority children. Ready schools use creative scheduling to make professional development activities available. They let parents and communities know about the importance of supporting these activities. They encourage teamwork among teachers.

6. **Ready schools introduce or expand approaches that have been shown to raise achievement.** Ready schools use education strategies backed by research evidence. Among such strategies are (a) providing prompt, supportive, intensive intervention before children fall behind, such as one-on-one tutoring and comprehensive school restructuring programs; (b) offering flexible, welcoming parent involvement opportunities; (c) offering flexible approaches to school and classroom organization, staffing, and grouping, such as (1) reducing class sizes to an average of 15 and helping teachers adjust to it, (2) adding paraprofessionals to the classroom, or (3) using mixed-age groupings; and (d) conducting and supporting educational research in the school.

7. **Ready schools are learning organizations that alter practices and programs if they do not benefit children.** Ready schools do not continue to engage in educational practices—such as retention in grade and providing extra-year programs—that have not been found to contribute effectively and consistently to children's development or learning. Seventy-three percent of elementary schools either retain children in kindergarten or place them in extra-year transition classes before or after their kindergarten year. In another ineffective practice, redshirting, parents delay their children's entry into kindergarten until they are 6 years old; because higher-income parents engage in this practice, the gap between rich and poor widens. Denying school entry to a child who meets the age requirement, in an

attempt to reduce individual differences, is ineffective. Another ineffective practice is pushing the curriculum of a higher grade down to a lower grade, particularly kindergarten, typically by teaching decontextualized letters and numbers.

8. **Ready schools serve children in communities.** Ready schools recognize the need to support other community services to meet the needs of children and families, especially health care and nutrition services. Some schools are hubs of health and human services. In other cases, community agencies or religious institutions provide these services. Either way, ready schools are extensions of communities, rooted in them. Neighborhood and community linkages may be infused throughout the curricula, and they may be shown by parents' strong decision-making roles in the school. Ready schools have ongoing, two-way relationships with social service and health agencies, making and following up on appropriate referrals.

9. **Ready schools take responsibility for results.** Ready schools challenge all children, setting high standards appropriate to every child. They target immediate assistance to children as soon as they fall behind. They assess children, so as to hold themselves accountable and get feedback to do their job better, and they share group assessment results with the community and individual results with each child's parents. Assessment techniques are appropriate to children's development; most of the time, observational assessment is preferable to paper-and-pencil tests. Another alternative is dynamic assessment, which makes use of computer technology to channel the assessment to the child's level.

10. **Ready schools have strong leadership.** School leaders sustain ready schools by their vision and agenda for the school. They are strong, articulate, and the clear source of leadership for instruction and other school activities. One individual may be the leader, or several may share leadership. School leaders make a clear, consistent public commitment to an achievable set of instructional priorities and create the climate for success.

They have the authority to make decisions, including budgetary ones, and they are visible and accessible to children, parents, and community members. They teach and mentor others.

School readiness is clearly the product of the marriage between early childhood programs and schools. It is a statement about the school's initial expectations for children's development and the child outcomes that have come to be expected of early childhood programs. This marriage took place because of the growing recognition that children learn a great deal in their early childhood years and that society can do much more to take advantage of this public investment opportunity (National Research Council, 2001). When policymakers invest large amounts of money in children, they do so primarily through the public schools. But with public attention comes public responsibility. Thus, early childhood policymaking and politics have joined education policymaking and politics.

CONCLUSION

Early childhood education—as practiced in the nation's child care centers and homes, and in Head Start, prekindergarten, and kindergarten programs—is not merely the transmission to young minds of the concepts of numbers, letters, shapes, and colors. It is our first public statement of the values we wish to pass on to our children. We say that we value personal initiative, collaborative problem solving, and tolerance and respect for others. These, then, are the values that should be evident in every setting where young children spend their time and have the opportunity to create their own futures.

REFERENCES

Alwin, D. F. (1984). Trends in parental socialization values: Detroit, 1958–1983. *American Journal of Sociology, 90*(2), 359–382.

American Educational Research Association, American Psychological Association, & National Council on Measurement in Education. (1999). *Standards for educational and psychological testing.* Washington, DC: American Psychological Association.

Arnett, J. (1989). Caregivers in day-care centers: Does training matter? *Journal of Applied Developmental Psychology, 10*(4), 541–552.

Baumrind, D. (1971). Current patterns of parental authority. *Developmental Psychology Monograph, 4*(4, Part 2).

Bureau of the Census, U.S. Department of Commerce. (n.d.). *Historical poverty tables, Current Population Survey,* Annual Social and Economic Supplements. Poverty and Health Statistics Branch, HHES Division. Retrieved September 27, 2002, from *http://www.census.gov/hhes/ poverty/histpov/hstpov20.html.*

Bureau of Labor Statistics, U.S. Department of Labor. (2002a). *2000 National Occupational Employment and Wage Estimates.* Retrieved July 23, 2002, from *http://www.bls.gov/oes/2000/oes_nat.htm.*

Bureau of Labor Statistics, U.S. Department of Labor. (2002b). *Working in the 21st Century.* Retrieved September 26, 2002, from *http://www.bls.gov/opub/working/page16b.htm.*

Campbell, F. A., Pungello, E. P., Miller-Johnson, S., Burchinal, M., & Ramey, C. T. (2001). The development of cognitive and academic abilities: Growth curves from an early childhood educational experiment. *Developmental Psychology, 37,* 231–242.

Cauthen, N., Knitzer, J., & Ripple, C. (2000). *Map and track 2000: State initiatives for young children and families.* Retrieved November 5, 2003, from Columbia University, National Center for Children and Poverty Web site: *http://www.nccp.org/pub__mat00.html.*

Ceglowski, D., & Bacigalupa, C. (2002, Spring). Keeping current in child care research annotated bibliography: An update. *Early Childhood Research & Practice, 4*(1). Retrieved October 3, 2002, from *http://ecrp.uiuc.edu/ v4n1/ceglowski.html.*

Committee for Economic Development, Research and Policy Committee. (1985). *Investing in our children.* Washington, DC: Author.

Dodge, D. T., Colker, L., & Heroman, C. (2002). *The Creative Curriculum for preschool* (4th ed.). Washington, DC: Teaching Strategies, Inc.

Education Commission of the States. (2000). *ECS tools and resources: Pre-kindergarten database.* Retrieved September 27, 2002, from *http://www.ecs.org/clearinghouse/27/24/2724.htm.*

Education Commission of the States. (2002). *State-funded pre-kindergarten programs: States requiring a bachelor's degree for pre-kindergarten teachers.* Retrieved October 2, 2002, from *http://www.ecs.org/dbsearches/Search_Info/EarlyLearningReports.asp?tbl=table11.*

Egertson, H. (1987, May 20). Reclaiming kindergarten for 5-year-olds. *Education Week, 6*(34), 28, 19.

Epstein, A. S., Morgan, G., Curry, N., Endsley, R., Bradbard, M., & Rashid, H. (1985). *Quality in early childhood programs: Four perspectives* (High/Scope Early Childhood Policy Papers, 3). Ypsilanti, MI: High/Scope Press. (ERIC Document ED 262/903).

Epstein, A. S. (1993). *Training for quality: Improving early childhood programs through systematic inservice training.* (Monographs of the High/Scope Educational Research Foundation, 9.) Ypsilanti, MI: High/Scope Press.

Goal 1 Resource and Technical Planning Group. (1993). *Reconsidering children's early development and learning: Toward common views and vocabulary.* Report to the National Education Goals Panel. Retrieved October 4, 2002, from the National Education Goals Panel Web site: *http://www.negp.gov/Reports/child-ea.htm.*

Harms, T., Clifford, R. M., & Cryer, D. (1998). *Early Childhood Environment Rating Scale* (Rev. ed.). New York: Teachers College Press.

Head Start Bureau, U.S. Department of Health and Human Services. (2000). Using child outcomes in program self-assessment. Information Memorandum ACYF-IM-HS-00-18. Retrieved November 5, 2003, from *http://www.assessmenttech.com/pages/guidelines/ACFMemo.html.*

Head Start Bureau, U.S. Department of Health and Human Services. (2002). *2002 Head Start fact sheet.* Retrieved November 5, 2003, from *http://www.acf.hhs.gov/programs/hsb/research/2003.htm.*

High/Scope Educational Research Foundation. (2002). *Child Observation Record for Infants and Toddlers.* Ypsilanti, MI: High/Scope Press.

High/Scope Educational Research Foundation. (2003a). *Preschool Child Observation Record* (2nd ed.). Ypsilanti, MI: High/Scope Press.

High/Scope Educational Research Foundation. (2003b). *Preschool Program Quality Assessment* (2nd ed.). Ypsilanti, MI: High/Scope Press.

Hohmann, M., & Weikart, D. P. (2002). *Educating young children: Active learning practices for preschool and child care programs* (2nd ed.). Ypsilanti, MI: High/Scope Press.

Howes, C. (1997). Children's experiences in center-based child care as a function of teacher background and adult-child ratio. *Merrill-Palmer Quarterly, 43,* 404–425.

Hunt, J. Mc V. (1961). *Intelligence and experience.* New York: Ronald Press.

Kamii, C. (1986, September). Autonomy vs. heteronomy. *Principal, 66*(1), 68–70.

Karnes, M. B., Schwedel, A. M., & Williams, M. B. (1983). A comparison of five approaches for educating young children from low-income homes. In Consortium for Longitudinal Studies, *As the twig is bent . . . Lasting effects of preschool programs* (pp. 133–170). Hillsdale, NJ: Erlbaum.

Kim, Y. K. (1987, June). *Parent and Child Program evaluation report.* Lexington, KY: University of Kentucky Department of Educational and Counseling Psychology, and Interdisciplinary Human Development Institute.

Lazar, I., Darlington, R., Murray, H., Royce, J., & Snipper, A. (1982). Lasting effects of early education. *Monographs of the Society for Research in Child Development, 47*(2–3, Serial No. 195).

Love, J. M., Logue, M. E., Trudeau, J. V., & Thayer, K. (1992). *Transitions to kindergarten in American schools: Final report of the National Transition Study.* Washington, DC: U. S. Department of Education.

Marcon, R. (2002). Moving up the grades: Relationship between preschool model and later school success. *Early Childhood Research & Practice, 4*(1). Retrieved February 13, 2003, from *http://ecrp.uiuc.edu/v4n1/marcon.html.*

McKey, R. H. (2003). The Head Start Family and Child Experiences Survey (FACES): What are we learning about program quality and child development? *Children and Families, 17*(1), 62–64. Retrieved February 13, 2003, from *http://www.acf.hhs.gov/programs/core/ongoing_research/faces/nhsa/nhsa_faces_w03.pdf.*

McKey, R. H., Condelli, L., Ganson, H., Barrett, B., McConkey, C., & Plantz, M. (1985, June). *The impact of Head Start on children, families, and communities* (Final report of the Head Start Evaluation, Synthesis, and Utilization Project). Washington, DC: CSR.

Meisels, S. J. (1994). *Developmental screening in early childhood: A guide* (4th ed.). Washington, DC; NAEYC.

Miller, L. B., & Bizzell, R. P. (1984). Long-term effects of four preschool programs: 9th and 10th grade results. *Child Development, 55,* 1570–1587.

Montessori, M. (1967). *The absorbent mind.* New York: Holt, Rinehart, and Winston.

National Association for the Education of Young Children. (1997). NAEYC position statement on developmentally appropriate practice in early childhood programs serving children from birth to age 8. In S. Bredekamp & C. Copple (Eds.), *Developmentally appropriate practice in early childhood programs* (Rev. ed.). Washington, DC: National Association for the Education of Young Children.

National Association for the Education of Young Children. (1998). *Accreditation criteria & procedures of the National Academy of Early Childhood Programs.* Washington, DC: Author.

National Center for Education Statistics, U.S. Department of Education. (2001). Table 64—Public elementary and secondary pupil/teacher ratios, by level, type, and enrollment size of school: Fall 1987 to fall 1999, Common core of data surveys. Retrieved December 13, 2002, from *http://nces.ed.gov/pubs2002/digest2001/tables/PDF/table064.pdf.*

National Education Goals Panel. (1991). *Building a nation of learners.* Retrieved October 4, 2002, from *http://www.negp.gov/.* First goal specified at *http://www.negp.gov/page3-3.htm.*

National Research Council. (2001). *Eager to learn: Educating our preschoolers.* Committee on Early Childhood Pedagogy. B.T. Bowman, M.S. Donovan, & M.S. Burns (eds.). Commission on Behavioral and Social Sciences and Education. Washington, DC: National Academy Press. Retrieved October 4, 2002, from *http://www.nap.edu/books/0309068363/html/.*

National Research Council and Institute of Medicine (2000). *From neurons to neighborhoods: The science of early childhood development.* Committee on Integrating the Science of Early Childhood Development. J. P. Shonkoff & D. A. Phillips (eds.). Board on Children, Youth, and Families, Commission on Behavioral and Social Sciences and Education. Washington,

DC: National Academy Press. Retrieved October 4, 2002, from *http://www.nap.edu/books/0309069882/html/*.

Phillips, D. A. (Ed.). (1987). *Quality in child care: What does research tell us?* Washington, DC: National Association for the Education of Young Children.

Piaget, J. (1932). *The moral judgment of the child.* London: Routledge and Kegan Paul.

Piaget, J. (1970). *Science of education and the psychology of the child.* New York: Orion Press.

Pierson, D. E., Walker, D. K., & Tivnan, T. (1984). A school-based program from infancy to kindergarten for children and their parents. *The Personnel and Guidance Journal, 62,* 448–455.

Proctor, B. D., & Dalaker, J. (2002). *Poverty in the United States: 2001.* U.S. Census Bureau, Current Population Reports, P60–219. Washington, DC: U.S. Government Printing Office. Retrieved September 27, 2002, from *http://www.census.gov/prod/2002pubs/p60-219.pdf*.

Puckett, M. B., & Black, J. K. (1999). *Authentic assessment of the young child: Celebrating development and learning* (2nd ed.). New York: Prentice Hall.

Reynolds, A. J., Temple, J. A., Robertson, D. L., & Mann, E. A. (2001). Long-term effects of an early childhood intervention on educational achievement and juvenile arrest: A 15-year follow-up of low-income children in public schools. *Journal of the American Medical Association, 285,* 2339–2346.

Ruopp, R., Travers, J., Glantz, F., & Coelen, C. (1979). *Children at the center: Summary findings and policy implications of the National Day Care study,* Vol. 1. Cambridge, MA: Abt Associates.

Schulman, K., Blank H., & Ewen, D. (1999). *Seeds of success, state pre-kindergarten initiatives 1998–1999,* executive summary. Washington, DC: Children's Defense Fund. Retrieved October 9, 2002, from *http://www.childrensdefense.org/pdf/seeds_of_success.pdf*.

Schweinhart, L. J., Barnes, H. V., & Weikart, D. P. (1993). *Significant benefits: The High/Scope Perry Preschool study through age 27.* (Monographs of the High/Scope Educational Research Foundation, 10). Ypsilanti, MI: High/Scope Press.

Schweinhart, L. J., & Weikart, D. P. (1997). The High/Scope Preschool Curriculum Comparison Study through age 23. *Early Childhood Research Quarterly, 12,* 117–143.

Shore, R. (1998). *Ready schools*. A report of the Goal 1 Ready Schools Resource Group. Washington, DC: National Education Goals Panel. Retrieved November 5, 2003, from *http://www.negp.gov/Reports/readysch.pdf.*

Smith, K. (2002). *Who's minding the kids? Child care arrangements: Spring 1997.* Current Population Reports pp. 70–86. Washington, DC: U. S. Census Bureau.

Spodek, B., & Saracho, O. (Eds.). (1996). *Issues in early childhood educational assessment and evaluation, Yearbook in early childhood education, 7.* New York: Teachers College Press.

U.S. Congress. (1997). Individuals with disabilities education amendments of 1997. Retrieved October 8, 2002, from *http://www.ideapolicy.org/Relaunch/law.htm.*

U.S. Congress. (1998). Community opportunities, accountability, and training and educational services act of 1998. Public Law 105–285. Retrieved November 5, 2003, from *http://frwebgate.access.gpo.gov/cgi-bin/useftp.cgi?IPaddress=162.140.64.21&filename=publ285.pdf&directory=/diskc/wais/data/105_cong_public_laws.*

Weikart, D. P., & Schweinhart, L. J. (1999). The High/Scope Curriculum for early childhood care and education. In J. L. Roopnarine & J. E. Johnson (Eds.), *Approaches to early childhood education* (3rd ed.). Columbus, OH: Merrill.

Whitebook, M., Howes, C., & Phillips, D. (1998). *Who cares: Child care teachers and the quality of care in America.* Final report of the National Child Care Staffing Study. Oakland, CA: Child Care Employee Project.

Zill, N., & Resnick, G. (2002a). Relationships of teacher beliefs and qualifications to classroom quality in Head Start. Presentation at Head Start's 6th National Research Conference, Washington, DC. Retrieved February 13, 2003, from *http://www.acf.hhs.gov/programs/core/ongoing_research/faces/faces_pres_papers.html.*

Zill, N., & Resnick, G. (2002b). Constancy and change in Head Start classroom quality and school readiness gains. Presentation at Head Start's 6th National Research Conference, Washington, DC. Retrieved February 13, 2003, from *http://www.acf.hhs.gov/programs/core/ongoing_research/faces/faces_pres_papers.html*

Zill, N., Resnick, G., Kim, K., O'Donnell, K., Sorongon, A., McKey, R. H., et al. (2003, May). *Head Start FACES 2000: A whole-child perspective on program performance.* Fourth Progress Report. Washington, DC: Child Outcomes Research and Evaluation and the Head Start Bureau, Administration for Children and Families, U.S. Department of Health and Human Services. Retrieved November 26, 2003, at *http://www.acf.hhs.gov/ programs/core/ongoing_research/faces/faces_pubs_reports.html.*

APPENDIX A
THE HIGH/SCOPE PERRY PRESCHOOL STUDY

Adults born in poverty who participated in a high-quality preschool program emphasizing child-initiated learning activities at ages 3 and 4 have half as many criminal arrests, higher earnings and property wealth, and greater commitment to marriage, according to the age-27 findings of the High/Scope Perry Preschool Study. Over participants' lifetimes, the public is receiving an estimated $7.16 for every dollar originally invested.

Conducted by the High/Scope Educational Research Foundation of Ypsilanti, Michigan, the study examines the lives of 123 African Americans born in poverty and at high risk of failing in school. At ages 3 and 4, these individuals were randomly divided into a group who received a high-quality, active learning preschool program and a group who received no preschool program. At age 27, 95% of the original study participants were interviewed, with additional data gathered from their school, social services, and arrest records. Subsequent group differences represent preschool program effects. Findings reported herein were statistically significant (with a two-tailed probability of less than 1 in 20). The U.S. Department of Health and Human Services and the Ford Foundation funded the age-27 phase of the study. Major findings are shown in Figure 2 and summarized below.

Social responsibility. By age 27, only one fifth as many program group members as no-program group members were arrested 5 or more times (7% vs. 35%), and only one third as many were ever arrested for drug dealing (7% vs. 25%).

Earnings and economic status. At age 27, four times as many program group members as no-program group members earned $2,000 or more per month (29% vs. 7%). Almost three times as many owned their own homes (36% vs. 13%) and over twice as many owned two cars (30% vs. 13%). Three fourths as many of them received welfare assistance or other social services at some time as adults (59% vs. 80%).

Figure 2

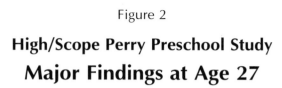

High/Scope Perry Preschool Study
Major Findings at Age 27

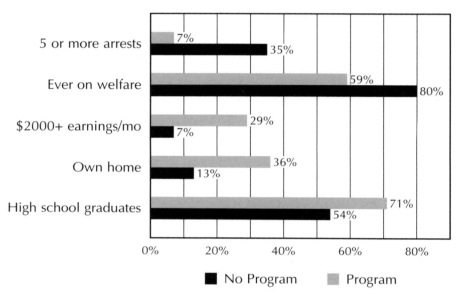

Educational performance. One third again as many program group members as no-program group members graduated from regular or adult high school or received General Educational Development certification (71% vs. 54%). Earlier, the program group had a significantly higher average achievement score at age 14 and literacy score at age 19 than the no-program group.

Commitment to marriage. Although the same percentages of program males and no-program males were married at age 27 (26%), the married program males were married nearly twice as long as the married no-program males (averages of 6.2 years vs. 3.3 years). Five times as many program females as no-program females were married at the age-27 interview (40% vs. 8%). Program females had only about two thirds as many out-of-wedlock births as did no-program females (57% of births vs. 83% of births).

Return on investment. A benefit-cost analysis (summarized in Figure 3) was conducted by estimating the monetary value of the program and its effects in constant 2001 dollars discounted annually at 3%. Dividing the $105,324 in benefits per participant by the $14,716 in cost per participant results in a benefit-cost ratio of 716% of the program investment returned to the public. The program was an extremely good economic investment, better than the stock market during the same period of time. The program's teachers were certified public school teachers who made weekly home visits. By increasing the number of children per teacher from 5 to 8, the program's cost per child per year could be reduced to $5,398—less than the average cost of Head Start programs in 2001—with no necessary loss in quality or benefits.

Figure 3

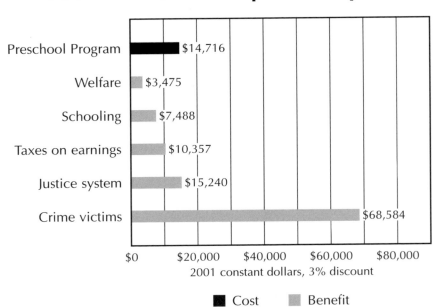

High/Scope Perry Preschool Study
Public Costs/Benefits per Participant

Implications. The High/Scope Perry Preschool study and similar studies suggest that high-quality early childhood programs have significant benefits because they:

- **Empower children,** by encouraging them to initiate and carry out their own learning activities and make independent decisions

- **Empower parents,** by bringing them into full partnership with teachers in supporting their children's development

- **Empower teachers,** by providing them with systematic inservice training in a validated educational model, as well as supervision and observational assessment tools that support this model

These findings demonstrate just how much high-quality early childhood programs can achieve. Because Head Start and other preschool programs have served only a fraction of the children living in poverty, and because the quality of these programs has varied, the nation has been losing the recoverable human and financial potential of its most vulnerable citizens. It is essential that the nation invest fully in high-quality preschool programs emphasizing child-initiated learning activities for all children living in poverty or otherwise at risk of failing in school.

Appendix B
National Information Sources on Early Childhood Programs

Bank Street College of Education
610 West 112th Street
New York, NY 10025-1898
(212) 875-4400
www.bankstreet.edu

Children's Defense Fund
25 E Street, NW
Washington, DC 20001
(202) 628-8787
www.childrensdefense.org

Education Commission of the States
700 Broadway, #1200
Denver, CO 80203-3460
(303) 299-3600
www.ecs.org

High/Scope Educational Research Foundation
600 North River Street
Ypsilanti, MI 48198
(734) 485-2000
www.highscope.org

National Association for the Education of Young Children
1509 16th Street NW
Washington, DC 20036
(800) 424-2460 or (202) 232-8777
www.naeyc.org

National Association of State Boards of Education
277 South Washington Street, Suite 100
Alexandria, VA 22314
(703) 684-4000
www.nasbe.org

National Black Child Development Institute
1101 15th Street NW
Suite 900
Washington, DC 20005
(202) 833-2220
http://www.nbcdi.org

National Conference of State Legislatures
7700 East First Place
Denver, CO 80230
(303) 364-7700
http://www.ncsl.org

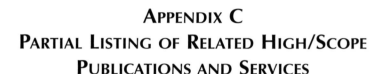

Appendix C
Partial Listing of Related High/Scope Publications and Services

High/Scope Press
High/Scope Educational Research Foundation
600 North River Street
Ypsilanti, MI 48198
U.S. Orders: 1-800-40-PRESS; Fax 1-800-442-4FAX
International Orders: 1-734-482-6660; Fax 1-734-482-6757
Online Store: *http://www.highscope.org*

Newsletters

Extensions, newsletter of the High/Scope Curriculum, 6 issues a year

High/Scope ReSource, published three times a year, no charge

Research

Into Adulthood: A Study of the Effects of Head Start, $29.95

Lasting Differences: The High/Scope Preschool Curriculum Comparison Study Through Age 23, $19.95

Lives in the Balance: Age 27 Benefit-Cost Analysis of the High/Scope Perry Preschool Program, $19.95

Models of Early Childhood Education $29.95

Significant Benefits: The High/Scope Perry Preschool Study Through Age 27, $25.95

Training for Quality: Improving Early Childhood Programs Through Systematic Inservice Training, $19.95

What Should Young Children Learn? Teacher and Parent Views in 15 Countries, $29.95

Assessment

Preschool Child Observation Record (COR), Second Edition, $174.95

Preschool Child Observation Record (COR) for Infants and Toddlers $149.95

Preschool Program Quality Assessment (PQA), Second Edition, starter pak $25.95

Preschool Educational Model

Daily Planning Around the Key Experiences: The Teacher's Idea Book 1, $19.95

Educating Young Children: Active Learning Practices for Preschool and Child Care Programs, Second Edition, $42.95

The Essential Parent Workshop Resource: The Teacher's Idea Book 4, $25.95

Fee, Fie, Phonemic Awareness—130 Prereading Activities for Preschoolers, $25.95

Letter Links—Alphabet Learning With Children's Names, $25.95

Making the Most of Plan-Do-Review: The Teacher's Idea Book 5, $25.95

Planning Around Children's Interests: The Teacher's Idea Book 2, $25.95

Preschool Readers and Writers: Early Literacy Strategies for Teachers, $34.95

100 Small-Group Experiences: The Teacher's Idea Book 3, $25.95

Study Guide to Educating Young Children: Exercises for Adult Learners, Second Edition, $19.95

Supporting Young Artists, $36.95

Supporting Young Learners: Ideas for Preschool and Day Care Providers, $29.95

Supporting Young Learners 2: Ideas for Child Care Providers and Teachers, $29.95

Supporting Young Learners 3: Ideas for Child Care Providers and Teachers, $29.95

You Can't Come to My Birthday Party! Conflict Resolution With Young Children, $34.95

High/Scope Preschool Key Experiences Series, Booklets and Videos

Classification, Seriation, and Number (Early Math), $9.95 (Booklet); $30.95 (Video); $34.95 (Set)

Creative Representation, $9.95 (Booklet); $30.95 (Video); $34.95 (Set)

Initiative and Social Relations, $9.95 (Booklet); $30.95 (Video); $34.95 (Set)

Language and Literacy, $9.95 (Booklet); $30.95 (Video); $34.95 (Set)

Space and Time (Early Math), $9.95 (Booklet); $30.95 (Video); $34.95 (Set)

Elementary Educational Model

85 Engaging Movement Activities—Learning on the Move , Grades K–6, $34.95

75 Ensemble Warm-Ups: Activities for Bands, Choirs, and Orchestras, Learning on the Move, Grades 4–12, $34.95

Foundations in Elementary Education: Guide and video, $15.95

Foundations in Elementary Education: Movement, $39.95

Foundations in Elementary Education: Music, $39.95

Language & Literacy, $29.95

Learning Environment, $29.95

Literature-Based Workshops for Language Arts—Ideas for Active Learning, Grades K–2, $34.95

Literature-Based Workshops for Mathematics—Ideas for Active Learning, Grades K–2, $34.95

Mathematics, $29.95

Science, $29.95

FOR PARENTS

All About High/Scope—A series of 10 information-packed fact sheets, 25 copies each of 10 fact sheets, $117.95, 25 copies of one fact sheet, $14.95

Helping Your Preschool Child Become a Reader, $4.95; Spanish version (*Ayudando a su Preescolar a ser un Lector: Ideas para Los Padres*), $4.95

You & Your Child Parent Newsletter Series, 25 copies each of all 12 newsletters, $130.95, 25 copies of one newsletter, $12.95

AUDIOVISUAL MEDIA

Elementary Video Package, 4 videos: *Active Learning, Classroom Environment, Language & Literacy,* and *Mathematics,* $30.95 each, $104.00 a set

10 Preschool Key Experience Posters, $29.95

Supporting Children in Resolving Conflicts, video, $49.95

Visiting High/Scope's Demonstration Preschool, 3 videos: *How Adults Support Children at Planning Time, How Adults Support Children at Work Time,* and *How Adults Support Children at Recall Time,* $22.95 each, $59.95 a set

TRAINING AND CONFERENCES

High/Scope offers extensive training courses for adults in the High/Scope educational model for infants and toddlers, preschoolers, elementary-aged students, and adolescents. Training options include one- and two-day workshops, week-long institutes, and multiple-week courses either at High/Scope Foundation headquarters in Ypsilanti, Michigan, or on site.

All High/Scope training is designed to provide concrete strategies and information that participants can take back to their own classrooms, centers, or homes. The lengthier teacher programs prepare participants to achieve full implementation of the High/Scope educational model in their classrooms or centers. The trainer programs prepare participants to train others in the model. **For more information, call (734) 485-2000, ext. 218, or e-mail** *training@highscope.org.*